THE NECESSITY
OF
WORSHIP

Written: by Patrick Pierre

All Biblical quotations were taken from the King James Version.

DEDICATION

TO
The Union Baptist Church Family,
Society Hill, South Carolina

WORSHIP IS A NECESSITY

THE NECESSITY OF WORSHIP
Written by Patrick Pierre

CHAPTER ONE

CALLING

One morning I as on my way to work, driving on a dark road while the town was asleep. Suddenly, I felt a quiet and pleasant Spirit invades my being. Immediately, I recognized the presence of God and wasted no time in giving Him what He had come to expect from me since the day of my conversion, according to the promise I did make, to worship God in season and out of season. I was compelled to pull over on the side of the road to allow the Spirit to usher me into worship. Inspired by God, I began to sing one of the many songs that I wrote.

Here I am, Lord, here I am.
Here I am, Lord, why don't you send me.
Here I am, Lord, here I am.
Here I am, Lord, ready to serve you.
I would do what you want me to do if you opened the doors of faith. I will walk in with your power and gladness ready to work.
Here I am, Lord, here I am
Here I am, Lord, why don't you send me.
Here I am, Lord, here I am.

Here I am, Lord, ready to serve you.
I would do what you want me to do,
I will tell the whole world
That you die on Calvary,
Just to save a sinner like me.
Here I am, Lord, here I am.
Here I am, Lord, why don't you send me.
Here I am, Lord, here I am.
Here I am, Lord, ready to serve you.
I will tell the whole wide world
About the man who gave sight to the blind.
Here I am, Lord, Here I am.
Here I am, Lord, why don't you send me.

Here I am, Lord, here I am.
Here I am, Lord, ready to serve you.
I would do what you want me to do.
I will tell the whole wide world,
There is power in your name,
And your Name is Jesus Christ.

After singing, I had a vision, and the Spirit ushered me into a room designed for worshippers. The thing that impressed me the most was that all the worshippers were worshipping God in their way. There was no sign of jealousy, envy, or malicious criticism.

They were worshiping in Spirit and truth with great respect for each other. They also respected each different diverse ways of worshipping the true and living God. In that room and in that moment, God was the center of worship. The Glory of the Lord emanated the room. Then, the Spirit instructed me to grab a pen and demanded that I write a manuscript on Worship. I said, "Lord, I will do what you want me to do if you opened the doors of faith." Right then, I developed a Gideon Spirit by throwing a fleece to God.

All-day extended my mind was on worship. Many questions crossed my intellect, am I worthy of writing concerning worship? Why have you chosen me? God seemingly ignored my questions. Therefore, I thought I had found a way to buy more time before writing this manuscript because I was writing a novel. I had estimated that it would take a year to complete the book before starting something else. However, God has a way of confirming His message to His children. That evening when I arrived home from work, I greeted Joy, my wife. We spoke briefly then I left so she could continue editing the new novel she just finished. I did not discuss anything with her concerning my fellowship with God that morning. I glanced over my shoulder at my wife because I perceived she was looking at me. Finally, she said, "Honey, I think you need to write a book concerning Spiritual matters such as worship. I looked up toward heaven and gave my God the biggest smile to say, "You are something else."

Immediately, I was convinced that the Spirit of God was compelling me to start teaching on worship in our Monday night Bible study. By God's grace, everyone who attended those classes enjoyed them, and blessings abound for my students as I taught this class; and I marveled as my God took His time as if he was saying: "I am with you all the way."

Before I go any further, there is a question that needs to be answered. That question is, "What is worship?" I will not dare answer that question without whispering a prayer to God.

My Prayer

Dear Lord, I am so thankful to be one of the vessels you have chosen to share with others on worship. Now, Lord, I depend on your dictation to show me what to write in answering the question, this I pray in your name Jesus Christ, "Amen."

According to some dictionaries, "To Worship" is to treat somebody as divine and show respect by engaging in acts of prayer and devotion." However, let us glance at a very familiar passage of scripture from the King James Version to establish a verdict or to eliminate some controversies; Jesus said in the gospel, according to John chapter 4:24, "God is a Spirit; and they that worship him must worship him in Spirit and truth." This verse does not leave us an option to worship God in any other way. The word of God has already determined this fact.

Worship expresses one feelings toward God by showing Him how deeply, excessively, and unquestioningly you love, admire, and respect Him.

To me, worship is indeed a personal love affair. Therefore, I daily demonstrate my deepest love and admiration for God through my tremendous and robust dedication, enthusiasm, and loyalty. These are not just lofty-sounding words, and there is significant meaning behind each of them love, admiration, commitment, and loyalty; you must be born again to develop these sentiments toward God.

Remember, the Bible says that there are only two ways you and I can worship God, and that is in Spirit and Truth. We worship in Spirit because God is a Spirit, and we worship in truth because He is the true and living God. However, only true believers can worship Him in that manner. Many people believe they are worshipping God when what they are doing is not true worship. They think that coming to church on Sunday is worship or that praying and asking God for blessings is worship, and they believe this because that is what they have been taught. However, I am not talking about those who worship Him in their ignorance because I used to be a member of that club. I will soon address this issue, but in the meantime, let us examine the requirements of worship. Nowadays, it seems as though it is just as hard as it was in the time of Jesus to find true worshippers.

God required these attributes back then, and He requires the same qualities today; the Bible says in John 4:23, "But the hour cometh, and now is, when the true worshippers shall worship the Father in Spirit and truth: for the Father seeketh such to worship Him." That is why I statedthat earlier only a true believer could worship God. In my opinion, there is a shortage of true worshippers because there is a shortage of true believers. A truer is totally submissive to God's word. After all, worship's fundamental is obedient and humility, while true worship cannot establish through disobedience and arrogance, which is a turn-off to God.

Some people never give God thought and go about life without a care of God's commandments until some major event happens in their life and they need God's favor. At those times, they have a sense of entitled blessing. That is arrogance. Throughout the Bible, we see the importance of worship, and often it is either demonstrating man's humility or observing man's arrogance regarding the subject. I declare unto that you, those who humble themselves before God never go wrong because they will frequently find that God is in their midst enjoying their worship, whether it is through ignorance or in knowledge.

CHAPTER TWO

WORSHIPING IN IGNORANCE

When I was in the sixth grade, it was a requirement for the school I attended in Haiti to take the students to church on Sunday mornings. The school was rigorous in this belief, and if one of the students missed a worship service on any given Sunday, he or she was required to bring an excuse in writing signed by their parents. As students, we did not have a choice but to pretend as if to act we loved and feared God when we were in the company of adult worshippers in the church, no one ever took the time out to explain to some of us the importance of worship, and they took for granted that we should have known. How could we have known if we were not taught? One Sunday, during worship, my friends, and I decided to play, and we were so wrapped up in our game that we forgot that our Principal's eyes were upon us. On Monday morning, the whole school finished the flag ceremony and the offertory prayer to God, our daily routine of morning worship. The principal asked my friends and me to remain in the schoolyard until everyone else entered their classrooms. Then, we remembered what we did, our sins flew before our eyes, and we started to cry because we knew that we were in trouble for playing in church. The principal pulled out his belt, beat us, and put us in detention for a couple of hours. At the end of our punishment, he told us, "Worshipping God is the most crucial privilege in a believer's life. It is not a time to play and be distracted but to show love, respect, and reverence to a true God. When my mother heard about shame forceful incident, so she called it, and the beating, she said that was not enough. She whipped me also. I was grounded for a week. I am so grateful to hear those golden words proceeded out of the Principals and Mother's mouths, making me the worshipper that I am today.

Again, God never has a problem with anyone who worships Him in their ignorance and will never reject them. He does not mind deploying a mentor who will introduce the inexperienced believer to the fundamentals of worship. However, the minute the worshipper k better, and God expects one to do better. That's why He opens the doors of knowledge. God is also well aware that ignorance spreads from one person to another as quickly as wildfires. He also understands the human tendency to reject Godly wisdom and to embrace ignorance willfully. However, we should keep in mind that God knows what God wants. He knows the way He wants it. Note that the type of worship that God expects from one person may differ from what He might expect from another. At the end of the day, if both are worshipping in Spirit and truth, God is pleased.

Believe it or not, most worshippers start out worshipping Him in ignorance because of a lack of training. However, I am sure that this statement does not fit Adam, the first man God formed. Adam was introduced to worship by God Himself. There was nobody to explain to him what was acceptable and what was not. Therefore, God instructed Adam to both forms of worship. As a free agent, he chose what was not permitted to God, and as a result, he was kicked out of Eden. God Himself banished Adam and his companion from the Garden of Eden. This experience entirely taught the first man Adam about the seriousness of worship. Adam had no other choice now but to follow the first and most crucial ingredient of worship: OBEDIENCE TO GOD.

Remembering disobedience to God is what drove Adam and Eve out of the garden, and compliance to God will bring them back into fellowship with God. After God introduced Adam to worship and praise, He anticipated man would teach one another to worship and praise, not praise, and worship. Let us keep in mind that God did not create Adam and Eve because He was lonely but to bring flavor to His garden, which He created for them. He proudly created man, listen to his tone in the process of designing, "And God said, Let us make man in Our image, after Our likeness: and let them have dominion over the fish of the sea, and over the fowl of the air, and over the graceful shame and over all the earth, and over every creeping thing that creepeth upon the earth." Genesis 1:26.

This verse alone stands tall to refute any idea, such as to the reason for God creating man, and it was not because He was lonely. From my understanding, He was speaking or having fellowship with another Supreme Being during the creation of man because God said, "Let us make man...

Another thing about God He does not mind praising His own work. The Bible says, "And God saw everything that He had made, and, behold, it was good. And the evening and the morning were the sixth day." Genesis 1:31

In addition, He does not mind praising His work just for training's sake. The word of God said again, "And God blessed the seventh day, and sanctified it: because that in it He had rested from all His work which God created and made." Genesis 2:3

I do not doubt in my mind that Adam and Eve introduced Cain and Abel to worship and praise. They had to. Because of the Garden of Eden experience, they learned how essential those two things were because praise, when sincere, gets God's attention. However, Worship, if it does in Spirit and Truth, it melts the heart of God. To avoid all controversies, I will prove that Cain and Abel were well familiar with worship and praise.

However, before drifting away from any further, it is necessary to discuss a little about the greatest deception that Adam brought on himself. The act took place where he was supposed to dwell forever. He had dominion over everything under the sun. His rich vocabulary allowed him to name every living creature. God created him with the dust of the ground and breathed into his nostril, and he became a living soul. God even made a soul mate for him. God named him. Then God is the type of Father that He is planted a garden for them and called the place Eden so they could live freely and broadly. Adam and his wife were free to do whatever they wanted. They could eat almost anything they desired except for one restriction. God commanded Adam not to eat from one tree under any circumstances. Otherwise, he would experience death. Deep down in my heart, I believe our God took Adam, and showed him the tree that would add a few words to his vocabulary if he ate from it. Words like hiding, naked, cursed, sorrow, thorns, sweat, till the ground, flaming swords.

Any worshipper of God should understand what transpired in the garden between the serpent, the woman, Adam, and God. After carefully studying the situation, we should not have any other choice but to learn everything we can about obedience to God. The story in the garden proves many things to us, and that is how man was then and how he is now. Adam's story was just a preview of the stories of our own lives. His story revealed the ungratefulness and the arrogance of man. It also demonstrated how unsatisfied we could be amid satisfaction, and this is due to greed. How easy it is for us to worship and praise the blessings and forget all about God from "Whom all blessings flow."

In an orderly fashion, let us reiterate what we have learned from Adam's mistakes.

First of all, the Bible lets us know that God felt Adam's loneliness and decided to create a helpmate for him. In other words, God was introducing the institution of marriage. This helpmate formality makes me wonder, did God ever discuss with Adam how He would create the helpmate for him? Alternatively, did God, because He is God takes it upon Himself to do it without giving Adam an explanation? Now, you ask how in the world can we determine that since the Bible does not mention the discussion between God and Adam. We will ponder that later. In the meantime, we need to know and believe that God has never been the author of confusion. If you have any doubt let us read I Corinthians 14:33 "For God is not the author of confusion, but of peace, as in all churches of the saints."

God has thus far demonstrated creation, communication, explanation, teamwork, worship, and praise. His deity and leadership skills in all aspects of those terms have proven that God was then, is now, and will continue to be The True Architect of the universe.

Creation: Genesis Chapter 1
Communication: 2:16-17
Explanation: Genesis: 1:3-31
 Teamwork Genesis 1:26

Worship: Genesis 2:3
Praise: Genesis 1:31

In the first chapter of the book of Genesis, we learned how God created the universe. Realizing everything that He made was good. Then in the 26th verse of the same chapter, God decided to make man, "And God said, let Us make man in Our image, after our likeness: and let them have dominion over the fish of the sea, and over the fowl of the air, and over the cattle, and over all the earth, and over every creeping thing that creepeth upon the earth."

You see, God had a well-defined plan for Adam's life. Adam would come into being with all power in his hands as far as the animals and earthly kingdoms were concerned. In other words, everything living would be subject to Adam. I call that authority with a capital A. God had great expectations for Adam, but those expectations came with the price of obedience to God.

We know God created Adam but how did He do this? In the 2nd chapter of Genesis and the 7th verse lies the answer to our question; and it reads:

"And the Lord God formed man of the dust of the ground and breathed into his nostrils the breath of life; and man became a living soul."

Wow! Our God is worthy to be praised. He took dust and turned it into flesh, bone, artery, blood, muscle, and skin. Then with his breath, He made it come alive. Awesome! Then He, God, went along and planted a garden for Adam to reside and to live like a spoiled rich prince. You see, God made sure He created everything before Adam was even created. Here again, God demonstrated His Fatherhood skills by providing for Adam. His provision for humankind is one of the reasons we call God Our Father because He provides for us.

Now let us study a little bit the creation of his helpmate because God felt it was not good for man to be alone, so God brought the woman into being.

"And the Lord God caused a deep sleep to fall upon Adam, and he slept: and He took one of his ribs, and closed up the flesh instead thereof;" Genesis 2:21

Who can touch this? There is no one! Our God is amazing! I can't help myself; I have to brag about my God.

God could have used other means to create Adam's helpmate, but He preferred to take this route, and again, I wondered why? I often say in my Sermons,' and when I am counseling married couples, I believe that the reason God took one of the ribs from man to make the woman was where the rib is positioned in the body. God chose the rib so they could walk side by side as husband and wife and worship God the same way, side by side. I believe some husbands might prefer for their wives to walk behind them like lesser beings. Could that have been the reason, or was it just for awareness? Hum, I wonder! Perhaps God chooses this route so man could cleave unto his wife, and they could be one flesh. I have no problem with this belief because it fits well with the word of God. However, let us look at those questions a little further. Everything God does, He does it to teach and prepare us for a better future. The scientific world would not deny that the idea of putting someone to sleep to perform serious surgeries came from God, the First Surgeon who gave us the knowledge to do so, but the way He did it was miraculous.

Now God was about ready to present Adam with his wife, his confidant, and his worship and praise partner. The moment had arrived for Adam to worship and praise God for filling his emptiness. Let us see what happened:

"And the rib, which the Lord God had taken from man, made He woman, and brought her unto the man. And Adam said, thus is now bone of my bones, and flesh of my flesh: she shall be called Woman because she was taken out of Man." Genesis 2:22, 23

Was I wrong for thinking Adam was about to worship God and praise Him for the woman? Yes, I was. Listen to how Adam sounded above; instead of glorifying and praising God for filling his emptiness, oh no; he instead commenced upon praising himself by taking the credit for all that God does. Does that sound familiar to us? I guess "The apple does not fall too far from the tree." We, as descendants of Adam, have been guilty of the same thing at times. Until we come into the knowledge of acknowledging God first in everything, He does for us. We will continue to fall short in our worship and praise. God must be the center of our lives.

When we examine Adam's statement above, it clearly answers the question posed earlier. Did God discuss Eves' creation with Adam? There is every indication that Adam knew about the surgery that God performed on him. Otherwise, why would he say bone of my bones and flesh of my flesh? There is no doubt in my mind that God shared with Adam how he was going to create his helpmate. How do I conclude this? God enjoys communicating with His children. Everything God did then was in preparation for us to learn by example. The story in the Garden agreed that communication was one of the most excellent tools used by God to prepare us for worship and praise.

Adam's behavior in praising himself instead of praising God seemed to be different at first. Many people thought Adam was bragging about the beauty of the woman. However, upon further scrutiny, one could conclude that Adam was boasting when he said Eve was bone of his bones and flesh of his flesh because God took her out of him. Therefore, Adam called her, woman. He had the right to call her whatever he wanted to because he oversaw naming all living creatures. You see how powerful Adam was.

Now the woman also was formed. She and Adam had the same right. Remember this, she was not created by accident, nor was she made out of pity for the man's sake. Yes, indeed, she was the last creature to be created, but greater still, she was part of the plan to live on earth comfortably as well as Adam. How do I know she was an heir of the will? In Genesis 1:26, God gave us foreshadow of the woman when God said, "Let them have dominion," with a mission to multiply and replenish the earth. The statement clearly revealed there would be a female for Adam, not another man but a female, because God had already created male and female as far as the animal kingdom was concerned and they each had their mate. The best part about it was that not only did God create the animals, He also made them after their kind. I believe God did this to avoid a donkey from having a monkey for a helpmate or a dog from having a cat for a helpmate. Just a little levity, HUMM! God made sure that whenever He created a male, there was also a female. Again, God made sure everybody had a mate to maintain balance. God intended to introduce the first institution, which was the institution of marriage. Through it, He expected them to be fruitful and multiply the earth, which brings about the topic that is being debated in our communities today. However, according to the Bible, the same sex-couple was not in God's original plan as they are just not physically equipped to make this happen.

Going back to what I said before, the woman had the same rights as Adam, but she was limited in her knowledge of some of God's instructions personally to Adam face to face. The reason for the limitation was that she was not yet created. She learned that she had no other choice but to know it from

Adam as God did not address her. The man Adam in some instances, served as a mediator between God and the woman. Let us deal with this sensitive statement with an open mind, without accusing anyone of taking a side with the woman.

Before God taught Adam about choices, responsibilities, obedience, and consequences of sin, God made ready everything that Adam and his wife would need to live forever. Remember God placed Adam in the Garden of Eden to introduce him to the Edenite Covenant so that he would be steward over the Garden:

"And the Lord God took the man and put him into the Garden of Eden to dress it and to keep it. And the Lord God commanded the man, saying, of every tree of the garden thou mayest freely eat: But of the tree of the knowledge of good and evil, thou shall not eat of it: For in the day that thou eateth thereof thou shall surely die." Genesis 2:15-17

But where was the woman at this point? For some reason, God did not invite her to tag along with Him and Adam. Not only was she not a part of the most important conversation between God and Adam. Some may believe that even though they did not mention her name, she was by her husband's side that day. Not at all; that poor woman

24

was not even formed yet by God. Let us revisit Genesis 2:18, and you will see she was still an idea to God. If this is not enough, soon, I will rest my case as a factual point. However, another present Spirit eavesdropping in the conversation between God and Adam, even that sneaky Spirit knew the woman was not there.

After that, the man and his wife were both naked in the garden, and they were not ashamed. I could understand why they were at home enjoying life. The only person they had to answer to is God. He, God, did not have any problem with their nakedness. If it had been so, He would have dressed them. But as the story unfolded, we are introduced to a strange dialogue. This time it was not between God and Adam, nor between God and the woman. God had not said a word to the woman since He formed her, but it was the woman who was having a chat with a more subtle serpent than any beast of the field. Therefore, it was fit to be the right bait to entice the woman. It asked a question in a way that could plant a seed of doubt about God's word in her mind. It started with the word "Yea" to introduce the sentence of his question, "Hath God said yea shall not eat of every tree of the garden?" Genesis 3:1

25

The Spirit in the serpent was looking forward to something it did best, "a debate," and it found one. I am puzzled to find out why it went to the woman instead of the man. Was it the truth like many believe that he went to her because she was a weaker vessel? Time will answer the question soon. The woman will learn a lesson that some of us in today's world still can't grasp. Never debate with the devil; he lies! His question was very challenging:

"And the woman said unto the serpent, we may eat of the fruit of the trees of the garden: But of the fruit of the tree which is in the midst of the garden, God hath said, ye shall not eat of it, neither shall ye touch it, lest ye die." Genesis 3:2, 3

Her answers above acknowledged that she was not around when God commanded man not to eat from the tree in question. Why is that? She lied on God. He did say not to eat of the tree, but He never told Adam not to touch the tree, Genesis 2:16, 17. She reminds me of some of us who enjoy adding to the word of God to make it what we want it to be to serve our own purpose. You see again, "The apple does not fall far from the tree." The serpent bypassed the man and went to the woman because it perceived the man knew God's exact word. What made the

26

woman weak at this point was a lack of knowledge of the commandment. The serpent, in his persistency, went overboard to the end of calling God a liar to fool Adam and Eve. It assured her in a way that God was not telling them the truth about the consequences of eating from the tree. It said to her that they would not surely die if they ate of the tree. Genesis 3: 4

There was a side of God that the serpent and Eve never knew. Maybe they were only familiar with the loving kindness of The Creator. There would be a surprise coming their way. They misunderstood the Person of God just like we do today. We only see the good side of God and maybe that's the reason we talk so much about the devil as though he could possess those who are in God's hands, which, by the way, is impossible! Let us observe what he said to her: "For God doth know that in the day ye eat thereof, then your eyes shall be opened, ye shall be as God knowing good and evil." Genesis 3: 5

After the serpent spoke to the women, he accomplished his mission, and the woman was about to make her husband play the fool. I believed that something interesting happened to the woman. I think she broke the garden's rules by even carrying on such a conversation with the serpent. Let me make something clear; there is no record in the Bible of God instructing the first couple not to speak to anyone else. However, keep in mind that the conversation between the woman and the serpent was the first recorded communication she ever had with an interlocutor. From the beginning of the creation stage until the third chapter of Genesis, the Bible never mentioned the woman in a dialogue with God. I am insinuating that just by talking to the serpent, she did significant damage to her psyche. Some people may wonder where I am going with this. Let us take a glance at Genesis 3: 6, "And when the woman saw that the tree was good for food, and that it was pleasant to the eyes, and a tree to be desired to make one wise, she took of the fruit thereof, and did eat, and gave also to her husband with her; and he did eat."

When Eve talked to the serpent, she was already polluted and infected by sin before she ever ate the fruit. How do I conclude this? "And when the woman saw that the tree was good for food." This statement convinced me that the woman, starting to watch the tree after talking to the serpent and waiting for its maturity. Sin infected Eve instantly, or she would not have known the difference between a tree that was ready and one that was not. In the second part of the verse, "and that it was pleasant to the eyes," every single thing that God had created for them was pleasant. Pleasant was what they knew, and delightful was their lifestyle.

However, pleasing to the eyes meant temptation. Eve would not have experienced this type of temptation had she not been talking to the serpent. However, by the infectious words of sin that proceeded out of the serpent's mouth, she was tempted. Eve coveted the fruit of the forbidden tree. Temptation is nothing less than the product of sin. She experienced greed, living in a garden where everything was miraculously good, pleasant, and tasty. Still, she wanted more, or she would not have taken the fruit and eaten of it if her heart was right. Her eating of the fruit was the aftermath of the initial sin. The saddest part of the whole story was that when she gave it to her husband, he ate it as well. When he ate from the tree, he demonstrated his willingness to believe what the serpent had said over what God had said. Right there on the spot, sin made its triumphal entry into the world, and it would take worship and praise of God to get rid of it. I am not stating that prayer and praise alone can get rid of sin, but worship and praise will keep you in God's presence and chase evil away after knowing and believing in God. By the way, it is impossible to know and believe in God without true repentance of sins unto salvation. "And a tree to be desired to make one wise," the third part of the verse confirmed that Eve had also adopted the sin of Spiritual covetousness. She nourished in her heart the desire to be wise like God to know good and evil. She turned her desire to reality by pursuing her dream, and Eve ate from the forbidden tree. Another interesting thing happened after they ate the fruit. Their eyes were opened, and they became acquainted with shame. The first thing they realized was that they were naked and clandestinely tried to do something about their exposures, but in the cool of the day, the Bible said they heard God's voice walking in the garden. Another interesting point in chapter 3, verse 8, reveals that the man had messed up big time.

God officially changed the man's name to Adam. Up until that time, God had referred to him as the man; but when he called him in the garden after he ate from the tree, God called him Adam. How did Adam's name come about? Was it the result of sin? Well, the Bible contained many instances where God changes His servants' names. Knowing who God is, He always has a reason for everything that He does.

As far as Adam and his wife were concerned, let me inject here at this point the only name given for his wife was the woman. Therefore, Adam was the man, and Eve was the woman. "Adam and his wife hid from the presence of the Lord God amongst the trees of the garden."

Quite a shameful moment in our fore parents' lives was hiding from the presence of the Lord God. In the following verses, we saw that "God called Adam and He said unto him, Where art thou?"

Strange as it may sound, God did not call the woman, only the man who had received His commandment face to face. Adam had failed to obey God, but at least Adam was honest concerning his reaction hiding from God; he explained to God that he heard His voice in the garden. Fear fell on him. Adam knew that he was naked; therefore, Adam hid himself. Earlier I thought Adam was hiding himself to show respect toward God. I was wrong again because to show respect for God is to keep God's commandment, and he did not do that. He hid because of fear of God. Was not this something that Adam also learned through his newly found wisdom and knowledge?

"The fear of the Lord is the beginning of wisdom: and the knowledge of the holy is understanding." Proverbs 9 verse 10

Adam's explanation did not please God at all; how do I know this? Genesis 3:11 "And He said, who told thee that thou wast naked? Hast thou eaten of the tree whereof I commanded thee that thou shouldest not eat?"

God asked Adam two questions at the same time. He did not allow Adam to answer the first question, but the second question, shook every single nerve in Adam's body I believe. I can imagine a Spirit of guiltiness had overtaken Adam's total being. This is the type of guilt that would force anyone to look down instead of up because of shame.

What made things difficult for Adam and his wife was that they were in the presence of an omnipotent, omnipresent, and omniscient God. Adam and his wife were not acting as though they were familiar with the attributions of God. If they had known, they would not have hidden themselves from God. They would have automatically perceived that God was also present and saw everything they had done. God was right there when Eve was conversing with the serpent and watched them eat from the tree of knowledge good and evil. Even today, as far as sins are concerned, the average believers act just like Adam and Eve ignoring the fact that our God is indeed a powerful God, He is everywhere, and He knows everything. A thumbs up for King David, who said in Psalm 139: 7, 8 "Whither shall I go from Thy Spirit? Or whither shall I flee from Thy presence? If I ascend up into heaven, Thou art there: If I make my bed in hell, behold, Thou art there."

Marvelously, that is what I call: no place to run, no place to hide because my God sees everything. Given the knowledge of God's attributions and power, why did not God protect Adam from that tree? Yes, God did give Adam all the protection that he needed to live forever in the garden by telling and showing Adam in the entire garden one tree to refrain from eating. God shared with him why he should never eat the fruit from the tree in question because of the price tag, which is death.

Unbelievably in this scenario, God taught Adam his first lesson, in that the matter of doing good or evil would always be a matter of choice.

Nothing takes God by surprise; He knew Adam was going to mess up by choice. According to my last statement, one could conclude that Adam was set up by God Himself to disobey. How wrong would the thinking be? The author of the letter to the

Hebrews let us know in the 10th chapter and verse 26, "For if we sin willfully after that, we have received the knowledge of the truth, there remained no more sacrifice for sins,"

That sounds like Adam's case. He chose to do the contrary of what God told him not to do it. Now let us see how Adam tried to cheat his way out of the situation by offering God an alibi, which did not make any sense to God because He did not weave the consequences of the sin. Let us take a glance at Adam's answers, which drove me into curiosity. Genesis chapter 3 verse 12, "And the man said, "The woman whom Thou gavest to be with me, she gave me of the tree and I did eat."

Do we detect an attitude in Adam's answer? Was he demonstrating a sign of arrogance? Was he upset with Eve? One would think so by his answer. Did Adam know what he was eating? Sure, he did. Did Eve trick him into eating the tree? Why then did Adam blame Eve? Was Eve guilty for offering the fruit to her husband?

In my opinion, Adam had an attitude, and not only that, but he was also very arrogant. This type of behavior is often associated with sin, especially when guilty of disobedience or caught actively in the act of unethical behavior. He was only displaying the arrival of his sinful nature. Was that enough to classify his behavior as such? Yes, listen to how he answered the questions. Whatever happened to, "This is now bone of my bones, and flesh of my flesh," Genesis 2 verse 23. It was his right to brag and to love his wife. As a matter of fact, this is what God expects from all men, but when she started interfering in the works that God entrusted in him as an adversary of wrongdoing, he should have taken a stand for both himself and God; this statement holds for Eve as well. Too often, we find leaders who have trouble understanding that integrity is the heartbeat of their leadership.

In Adam's case, it appeared that the bragging and the honeymoon had come to an end, and they had entered a stage of "Every man or woman for themselves." Adam sounded like he was upset with Eve after realizing what he ate. Who do you think to believe this? Adam knew firsthand of the danger of the tree; besides, he was the leading free agent of the garden. It was no mystery to Adam concerning the tree, God had told Adam all about the tree, and Adam informed Eve. It was Adam's duty to obey God even if Eve chose not to. Instead, he decided to listen to his wife, who had listened to the serpent over God's direct commandment!

Adam knew what he was eating. Did Eve willfully trick him? No, I do not think so, but unknowingly yes, she did. Eve fooled herself into believing the words of a serpent because it presented itself to her as one who had her best interest, and God deceived her. She bought the idea, and sold it to her husband in her ignorance, and he bought it. Adam became the biggest fool among them the minute he ate the fruit. I cannot emphasize enough that the serpent was the one who tricked Adam. It did it by corresponding through Eve. If she alone ate of the tree, it would not have had the same effect. The serpent knew how contagious sin could be and how easy the persuasion to sin is. Eve did not do anything wrong by offering the fruit to Adam. It was up to him to say no and start informing her about what God said concerning the tree in question. Adam chose to yield unto temptation.

Now the same blaming game that played out in the garden is playing today in our society. Adam blamed God on the sly when he told God who gave him the fruit to eat. He blamed Eve, and Eve blamed the serpent, and God the Righteous who knows perfectly well the hearts of all living creatures because He designed them cursed the serpent.

I believe there were a few things that took the serpent by surprise. Firstly, even though it cost Adam and Eve the garden, the snake was the only one that God cursed besides the ground. I think the serpent would have rejected his mission if it had known the outcome of its actions that only he who would get cursed. Genesis 3, verses 14, 15. As far as Adam and Eve were concerned, God banished them from the garden due to their sins. There is nowhere in the garden story where one would find that God cursed Adam and Eve. However, He cursed the ground to make their lives harder and right after that, Adam had no other choice but to come up with another name for his wife. No longer would she be called a woman. Her earthly name would become Eve. After that, God himself taught them how to dress by manufacturing their coats with skins because they were still in the garden. Genesis 3 verse 16-21.

Secondly, I believe that the serpent thought God would allow them to remain in the garden even after the fall of man because of God's compassionate nature. In its limited knowledge, the snake was telling Eve the truth of what it thought was fact, but it was limited in knowing God's complete reaction concerning disobedience because it was, being a creature. What the serpent said to Eve was about the garden, but what he did not know for them to live forever, God had to leave them in the garden so they could continually eat from the tree of life. God decided to make a liar out of the serpent and teach Eve of the seriousness of covetousness, greed, and Adam the heavy fine of disobedience by introducing him to a new world requiring Adam to work to survive. Genesis 3 verses 22-24. Alas, God ushered Adam and Eve out of the garden and changed the lock by placing Cherubim and flaming swords on the eastern side of the garden to protect the tree of life. What an embarrassing moment this must have been for Adam. Since that day, he became the father of all humankind and the father of sin. Even the world where he once lived became sinful forever since then. Adam left us his children a wicked inheritance, which is death, which none of us can decline. In the book of Romans, the 8th chapter verse 12, Apostle Paul did a better job in explaining what I am trying to say "Wherefore, as by one man sin entered into the world, and death by sin; and so death passed upon all men, for that all men have sinned:"

Adam's deception in the garden has brought me to the conclusion that worship and praise to God is a "Must" it both reminds us from time to time how poorly we treat our God through sin, which leads us to repentance to receive forgiveness from God. Do not forget that worship and praise is a secret language spoken by a believer, and God is the only one that understands the language. No matter where you are, if you speak the language, God will surely answer. One more thing about the language, God knows it well based on the sincerity of hearts.

One night I was carrying on a revival meeting; I preached a sermon entitled "Guilty, we are all guilty." Throughout the service, there was a woman who was offering to God tearful worship. At the end of the sermon, I invited those that needed prayer to come to the altar. The same woman made her way toward me, crying bitterly, saying, "God, I have sinned greatly against you. I have done what you told me not to do, and please forgive me for my disobedience." She said Pastor Can I tell you what I did? I am so ashamed of myself. The minute she said that a quiet Spirit had invaded the church. Everyone's ears became wide open to hear her tearful confession. This reaction of the congregants was not strange to me because I know both sides of a congregational church, the noisy and the Spiritual side. I hurried up and stopped her by asking her the most important question concerning her sin in question, "Did you tell God about it already?" She said yes, and I replied, do not waste your time telling this congregation or me because we do not have that kind of power to cast your sin into the sea of forgiveness. You have done well by taking it to God through worshipping Him." Do you believe God forgives you? I asked. She said, "I know He did. He reaffirmed it to me just now." Happily, I replied to her, now we can help you praise God for the deliverance. Some of us praised God that night, as it was the Day of Pentecost. I also believed that night, many spectators left the church angry with me for stopping her from revealing the sin that she sinned against her God, but the true worshippers left happy for her breakthrough through worship and praise. There is one thing that I learned a long time ago that true worship could bring out true confession and repentance.

CHAPTER THREE

WORSHIP A FAMILY ORDINANCE

The Bible tells us that Adam and Eve had two sons. The oldest one was named Cain, a farmer, and the younger son's name was Abel. He was a shepherd. I believe their parents, through the supervision of God, trained the two boys spiritually. Remember when God drove their parents away from the garden, He equipped them with Spiritual knowledge. In other words, He taught them how to redeem themselves. God expected Adam and Eve to pass this teaching on to their children. I believe those boys knew about the price tag of sin, which is death, and for this reason, they knew the best way to make God happy was through worship.

Let us see how seriously Cain and Able took their worship, knowing God Himself was the Judge of their presentation to Him. He knew that they knew how to worship in the form of sacrifice. Before I venture any further, Cain and Abel's offerings to God can act as food for thought if we deal with this question. Is offering to God an act of worship? If it is, what can we offer to God?

Offering to God is indeed an act of worship. I can push the issue regardless of all controversies, and criticisms, which may come my way. Worship is all about offering and offering is one thing that connects a believer to God. Please keep in mind that I am not referring to the financial offering, which seems to dominate the mind whenever the ears hear the word offering in a worship service? I am not trying to eliminate finance as a form of worship either since it is. However, to answer the second question, the most important offering an individual can offer God is "SELF." The minute He searches the individual's heart and sees his sincerity and his devotion toward Him, He begins to introduce the individual to various forms of worship according to his faith. Total dedication pleases God to the highest. Psalm 29, verses 1, 2 gives us a better understanding; "Give unto the Lord, O ye mighty, give unto the Lord glory and strength. Give unto the Lord the glory due unto His name; worship the Lord in the beauty of holiness." However, it will be up to the believer to follow his heart and give God his best. Now I can play with words a little by saying that worship has become all about giving after offering "SELF" to God. Receiving or rejecting is a call only God can make because He knows the heart of man. He either accepts the offering with gladness or rejects it, depending on the condition of the giver's heart. Remember, we serve a God that gives good gifts to his children. For example, God gave us someone precious to Him to die for us as a way to reconnect to Him through worship.

I am getting ahead of myself through excitement. Let us re-join Cain and Abel's story. We need to enlighten on the term "Worship through ignorance." When Cain and Abel reached the maturity to worship and present sacrifices alone to God, they did. They were the first persons, according to the biblical account, to worship God. In the same history, we learned that God would not settle for anything as far as their worship was concerned, especially when He knew the qualifications of the worshippers. He did not play with Cain and Abel, and indeed, He will not play with us because "He has no respect of a person." He is fair in his judgments. However, let us not allow the word respect, the way it uses above fool us because God is known to respect those who worship Him in Spirit and truth. In addition, He has no respect for all false pretenders, those who worship Him with their hearts far away from Him. Again, worship is a heart thing, and anyone who worships God with a

43

pure heart will be honored by His presence. Here the Bible says,

"And the process of time it came to pass, that Cain brought of the fruit of the ground an offering unto the Lord. And Abel, he also brought of the firstlings of his flock and of the fat thereof. And the Lord had respect unto Abel and to his offering: But unto Cain and to his offering He had not respect. And Cain was very wroth, and his countenance fell." Genesis 4: 3-5

During my meditation on the scriptures above, a few opinions captivated my mind, and when I thought them through repeatedly, I realized that the Spirits of Cain and Abel still manifest themselves amongst believers today. That brings me to the conclusion that we have either a Cain Spirit or Abel Spirit in worship. That explains most of the confusion we are having in the church today. I know no one would admit that they are a partaker of a Cain Spirit. Everyone would instead associate their soul with Abel. When I take a closer look at the beginning of verse 5, "but unto Cain and to his offering he had not respect." It blows my mind until it forces me to examine my worship of God closely. From what I understand, not only did God have no respect for the offering that he brought, but God also lost respect for him as well for bringing Him such an offering.

The last thing I would wish on anybody, except for the devil, is for God to lose respect for them. Believe it or not, this is something that is happening every day in our society. Could we imagine how many people that the same thing is happening to them on Sabbath day or whenever worship service is ongoing? The reason for that may vary, but it is going to be a heart thing.

At this point, Cain was not pleased with God's decision. He acted like one who lost a contest after trying to outdo his opponent. I believe Cain's offering did not come from his heart but from his competitive mind, which often led to jealousy. I learned a long time ago that jealousy, whether secular or religious, cannot be hidden. It will show its actual color when the right opportunity presents itself. Cain was very angry not with himself but with God and Abel. How dangerous it is when a believer calls himself mad with God. I have often heard testimonials where believers made it known that they were upset with God. I never had the desire to know what it would feel like to be angry with God at one time or another. God forbid; I think it would be a scary feeling. If Cain were still around, he would have been agreed with me because he had firsthand experience, and it did not turn out well for him. In a little while, we will see what Cain behavior has cost him. Let us move on with the story.

God knew Cain was enraged, and He confronted Cain to reason with him. Let us see how God starts the dialogue with Cain in the fourth chapter of Genesis, verses 6 and 7 "And the Lord said unto Cain, why art thou wroth? And why is thy countenance fallen? If thou doest well, shalt thou not be accepted? And if thou doest not well, sin lieth at the door. And unto thee shall be his desire, and thou shall rule over him."

God asked Cain two questions, and he failed to answer either one; God spoke, and he kept his mouth shut. Still, God in all His mercy, showed him where he went wrong for future reference, but he was too angry to pay God any attention. This behavior cost Cain a lifetime of opportunities. He could have received forgiveness. What happened to Cain was a learning experience for all worshippers. Now, what have we learned? Give God our best to keep sin away from our doors.

Here we find Cain, who was his own worst enemy. Sins had taken over his heart, and there was no room for reason. However, he was dealing with a God that loved to reason with his children. Whenever this occurs, the doors of mercies become wide open for sinners who are willing to acknowledge their sins and ask Him for forgiveness. Isaiah the prophet shared with us in chapter 1 verse 18 what God's mercy is about: "Come now, and let us reason together, saith the Lord: Though your sins be as scarlet, they shall be as white as snow; though they be red like crimson, they shall be as wool."

Cain did not show any Spiritual remorse after violating the code of worship, which was being truthful to God. If he had repented with tearful eyes, he would have begged God for pardon, but arrogance had vetoed any sign of humbleness that could lead his heart to repentance of jealousy. Keep in mind that Spiritual jealousy is a disease that affects the heart and causes it to be rebellious and hateful. Don't you see, instead of Cain taking responsibility for his slothfulness, he preferred to take his failure out on his brother? He revolted against Abel while they were in the field and slew him. Now Cain is about to become acquainted with a few rules of life.

There is no such thing as a perfect crime, and spiritually speaking, anyone who commits a murder might get away with it before man, but not before God because He sees it all. Cain must have forgotten that our God is everywhere; because he thought he had covered his tracts by burying his brother in the ground. God is ubiquitous and was already at the crime scene. He asked Cain for Abel, his brother. Impertinently Cain answered God with a lie and tried to be smart with it. He turned around arrogantly and asked God a question. Let us read the conversation together. "And Cain talked with Abel his brother: and it came to pass, when they were in the field, that Cain rose up against Abel his brother, and slew him. And the Lord said unto Cain, where is Abel thy brother? And he said I know not: Am I my brother's keeper." Genesis 4 verse 8-9.

Did Cain honestly know who God is? In the final analysis, did he know God? These two questions seemingly appeared as a repetition. However, there is a difference between the two. Cain made the same mistake as his father did in another form. Remember, after Adam sinned, he went and hid from God because he was naked. Cain, on the other hand, when God asked him for his brother, Cain answered with an attitude and stated, "I do not know. Am I brother's keeper? Allow me to shed some light on the subject and keep in mind that Cain did not know who God actually was, but he did know God. Relax a little and grant me the opportunity to complete this analogy. If Cain truly knew who God was he would not have answered God the way he did. He would have automatically recognized that God is omnipresent, omnipotent, and omniscient.

Therefore, everything is plain and naked before God. To keep it accurate, Cain would not have killed Abel, his brother; and then try to destroy the evidence of the crime by burying the body, thus becoming the first murderer, had he known who God was. However, whose fault was it for Cain not to know who God was? I will tell you, and it was his fault needless to blame anybody else because God's rejection of his offering told the story. It is a dangerous game against the soul to take God for granted. When we learn what God expects from us, and we choose to do the opposite because we want to, we are taking Him for granted as well.

I believe Cain knew God to some extent, and he had a certain amount of respect for Him because he did try to observe the worship of God, however, with mediocrity. Some of us today are the same way. Some of us know God and believe in God for someone else but not for ourselves. Whenever we doubt God's capabilities in our lives, it only proves we do not know who God is.

Cain will finally understand who God is, but it will not be a pretty picture for him after he finally allows the knowledge to sink in. Was Cain insane when he murdered Abel? If so, can we associate the unworthiness of his offering to God with his insanity? Why did God, who sees and knows all things before they happen, not prevent Abel from being Cain's prey?

The way Cain slew Abel proved the murder was premeditated. It had nothing to do with insanity, even though the act Spirited by jealousy consumed him, but he chose to ride in that driving force. Insane, he was not. Everything about the crime was well planned, the meeting in the field, the bloodshed, the burial, and the lies.

We should never forget, that everything we see happen in the Bible is for our learning today. It is preparation as well as a warning. The way we apply it to our lives determines if we experience a healthy or unhealthy Spiritual life. We maintain awareness between the do's and do not, by observing and keeping the precept, which becomes the only life to live. God could have prevented Cain from killing Abel, but we would be ignorant of how dangerous jealousy can be in both the religious and the secular world if He had done so. I do not want to drift away too far from the conclusion of Cain's verdict, but I must take a few minutes to deal with the last question concerning Abel's death. When we follow the Bible closely, we see that since day one, God had a beginning and an ending for his creation, that there is nothing secret about the Bible. Everything is in black and white. However, it requires divine guidance to understand God's purpose for all recorded things in the Bible. Humanly speaking, the Bible started with the creation of the first man Adam, and it will end with the reign of the second Adam, who is our Lord and Savior Jesus the Christ. When Cain slew Abel, his brother, through the driving force of jealousy because Abel had pleased God with his offering.

The Bible is a Spiritual puzzle book, and those of us who can put the puzzles together patiently will be honorary guests at the marriage of the Lamb. Again, everything in the Bible, good or bad, is for learning because those things are still manifesting themselves among the obedient and disobedient. Let us now go back to the conclusion of Cain's criminal charges before the judgment seat of God.

Cain, the liar, thought that he had made a believer out of God because he used his lips not knowing that God is always looking at the heart of his interlocutor. Do not forget that the heart can be sincere and deceitful. Who can know it but God. He knew Cain was crooked, and He answered him in

Genesis 4 verse 10-12 "And He said, what thou hath done? The voice of thy brother's blood crieth unto me from the ground. And now art thou cursed from the earth, which hath opened its mouth to receive thy brother's blood from thy hand; when thou tillest the ground, it shall not henceforth yield unto thee its strength; a fugitive and a vagabond shalt thou be in the earth."

After reading the verdict of God to Cain, it recalled other familiar passages of scripture, which said, "Saying Touch not Mine anointed, and do My prophets no harm." Psalm 105: 15

As an observation, Cain and the snake that beguiled his mother had a lot in common. Both were deceitful, arrogant, jealous-hearted, liars, and God cursed them both. Nonetheless, I must leave that alone, the snake became the first animal to be cursed by God for interfering in a divine plan for the record. Cain was the first human being, and he will not be the last to be cursed by God for messing with His worshippers.

Wow! Cain met a God that he did not meet before, and he had no other choice but to know and believe who God is. Cain's sin against his brother was a sin unto death. He was beyond repentance. In a way, God had sentenced Cain to a slow death penalty through hunger and remorse by attacking his livelihood as a farmer. The curse that God had put on him was an ongoing one. Wherever he went, he would create trouble because that is what a fugitive and a vagabond Spirit do, jump from place to place and from church to church.

Let us look at Cain's pathetic complaint after receiving the wake-up call from God. He tried to enter a plea in Genesis 4 verse 13, 14 "And Cain said unto the Lord, my punishment is greater than I can bear. Behold, Thou hast driven out this day from the face of the earth; and from Thy face shall I be hid; I shall be a fugitive and a vagabond in the earth; and it shall come to pass, that every one that findeth me shall slay me."

According to those verses above, we also meet a new Cain. One who has a great improvement in his conversation with God Deep down in my heart, I believe Cain recognized his mistake, accepted his punishment even though he did not have any say in the consequences of his sins.

Reminiscently speaking, God does not have any problem forgiving us our sins when we repent because it is a promise, but God never promised to take the consequences of the sin away regardless of the outcome. The price tag is still death. Cain agreed with his

53

sentence, but he worried that everyone that met him might have a taste for his blood.

Was Cain a prophet? Please help me laugh at the question, which appears so bizarre, silly, and stupid. "There is no such thing as a stupid question." It does not matter how we feel about the question; it remains, was Cain a prophet? How in the world was he worried about others hurting him while he was the third person on earth? Was Cain referring to his parents as thinking they would slay him if they ever saw him again? Hum!

I do not recall in Cain's sentence having any clause that dictated his fellow man would execute him. Was he prophesying about his future? No, not at all; the man was far from being a prophet. It was the fear of dying that caused him to arrive at this conclusion. He was petitioning God for divine protection that would shield him from his fellow man. The way he ended his complaint seemed to reveal that other people were living in the land beside him and his parents because he said in the latter part of the verse, "and it shall come to pass, that ever one that findeth me shall slay me." He was not referring to his parents only when using the compound word everyone. However, he was speaking in the future tense. He knew about the mission that God had entrusted in his parents' hands "To be fruitful and multiply." Having children was the primary reason they created them. Adam will be the father, and Eve his wife, the mother of all humankind. Here comes the revelation, which can create much controversy among theologians, but let us remember that to agree or disagree is our prerogative. I believe the statement made by Cain at the end of his complaint referred to his family, other brothers, and sisters because by killing Abel, his brother, he had chosen to be an outcast. He would no longer be considered a member of the family. His action made it clear; he was at war with the family and all generations to come. The battle is still going on today. Therefore, many people today name their children Abel. When was the last time we met somebody named Cain? This is the residue of the curse.

Again, after Cain killed Abel, he had broken the family tie. He realized that God was the only one that could protect him. Cain knew that he disobeyed God and His covenant when he murdered Abel. I believe Cain was aware of the penalty for this sin because I am confident that God did not leave that stone unturned. It was one of the commandments "Thou shall not shed another man blood." Now, you might say that the Ten Commandments were yet to be written, and you would be correct. So, then you say, how do I conclude there was a covenant? Let us drift away from the subject matter to clarify these statements. Let us take a tour around the covenant God made with Noah after the triumphant arrival of the Ark in the dried ground. God made a similar covenant with Noah as He once made with Adam. In the case of Adam, involved a tree and with Noah, the preparation of the meat sacrifice was the subject matter, both required obedience. Let us read it for ourselves, "And God blessed Noah and his sons, and said unto them, be fruitful, and multiply, and replenish the earth. And the fear of you and the dread of you shall be upon every beast of the earth, and upon every fowl of the air, upon all that moveth upon the earth, and upon all the fishes of the sea; into your hand are they delivered. Every moving thing that liveth shall be meat for you; even as the green herb have I given you all things. But flesh with the life thereof, which is the blood thereof, shall ye not eat. And surely your blood of your lives will I require; at the hand of very beast will I require it, and at the hand of man; at the hand of every man's brother will I require the life of man." Genesis 9 verses 1-5.

This covenant could have served as a carbon copy of the one that God gave to Adam with some revisions. In Genesis chapter 9 verse 6, God said, "Whoso sheddeth man's blood, by man shall his blood be shed: for in the image of God made He man." Cain heard those words before. That was one of the reasons he answered God the way he did in his plaint. To God is the Glory. To prove another point, after the death of Abel, I believe that Adam even disowned Cain because Cain's name was not mentioned in the genealogy of Adam in Genesis chapter 5 before checking it out for yourselves, make sure to meditate a little in verse 3 which puts the icing on the cake.

Furthermore, for God not to lecture to Cain the same thing He preached to Noah, especially the sixth verse that would have meant that God had learned from the mistake of Cain slaying Abel. Therefore, He put a law in place to prevent the repetition of the same crime; this is a meaningless thought to think that way because God would not have blamed Cain for not knowing any better. Our God is well acquainted with the law of ignorance. That is the reason He offers amnesty, a plan to those of us who practice this law innocently.

Then He equips us with knowledge, understanding, and wisdom if we are willing to digest it, or prefer not to, we will answer our sins accordingly. Then, our ignorance would switch over into stupidity, and there are consequences when that happens.

Let us go back and look at the answers God gave to a Cain who was afraid of being slain by any man. In verses 15 and 16 of Genesis chapter 4, God profoundly displayed His mercy. He sent out an SOS on Cain's behalf. Let us take a look at it. It is beautiful, "And the Lord said unto him, therefore whosoever slayeth Cain, vengeance shall be taken on him sevenfold. And the Lord set a mark upon Cain, lest any finding him should kill him."

Quite a divine protection; in his guilty condition, God still answered Cain's prayer full of compassion. In my opinion, Cain had received a fair deal considering the seriousness of his crime. One thing is for sure God did not wave the consequences of his sin as far as him being cursed. The status of Cain being a fugitive and a vagabond had remained, but he was divinely protected from being slain, and this was a great demonstration of God's Mercy.

This is the end of the story, but we do need to establish the difference between the two offerings and what made God accept Abel's and reject Cain's.

When I was growing up, I met many different views concerning the two offerings. Ultimately, I never rejected some of the opinions. However, some of them are worth mentioning, and some are not. I have heard that God chose Abel's offering because he was the more youthful brother. God had a record that proved He preferred to bless the younger brother over the oldest. For example, with Noah's children, God chose Japheth over Shem; in Isaac's children Jacob over Esau; in Joseph's children, Manasseh over Ephraim; and in David's children, Solomon over Absalom. The law of agreeing and disagree are still in effect here. I am afraid I disagree with this theory because it is applying in the wrong context.

The next one was God rejected Cain's offering because it was not a blood offering; it was a fruit offering. Believe it or not, the popular belief is that Cain's offering was rejected, and Abel's was accepted because Abel offered a blood offering. I dare not put forth a resistance against that view because the author of the book of Hebrews, whether it is Apostle Paul or someone else, has backed up this view at least one hundred percent in chapter 9 verse 22 "And almost all things are by the law purged with blood;

and without shedding of blood is no remission."

However, the word "Almost" in verse above has authorized me to enter my point of view. I believe that Cain's problem was his heart which, in my opinion, was experiencing a lack of sincerity and purity to make an offering to our God, who pays more attention to the heart of the giver. According to Deuteronomy chapter 14 verse 22, 23, said "Thou shalt truly tithe all the increase of thy seed that the field bringeth forth year by year. And thou shalt eat before the Lord thy God, in the place which He shall choose to place His name there, the tithe of thy corn, of thy wine, and of thine oil, and the firstlings of thy herds and of thy flocks; that thou mayest learn to fear the lord thy God always."

Cain offered to God what he was supposed to provide as a farmer who grew produce. The law required individuals to offer God the first fruit of their substances. However, if the heart were not happy and sincere when giving to God, God would reject the offering, I believe. Nothing impresses God more than a cheerful giver. Apostle Paul said, "Every man according as he purposeth in his heart, so let him give; not grudgingly, or of necessity: for God loveth a cheerful giver." 2nd Corinthians" 9 verse 7.

Again, Cain had heart trouble when he prepared and presented his offering. He did not do it well at all. His reaction later toward God and his brother had proven that he had had a severe heart condition. In other words, Cain was a fool. (Proverbs 1:22)

Now let us discuss the subject of Cain's wife. Throughout my ministry, I find myself answering the questions who was Cain's wife? Where did she come from? Among the people who asked me, some of them were very honest in pursuing knowledge. Others had asked to open an argument with the intent to prove the immorality of the Bible. I never allow myself to fall into that trap. Where I come from, we have an old proverb that says, "To take a snake to school is one thing. To make it sit down is another thing." Believe it or not, this is one of the most straightforward questions to answer. Cain married one of his sisters because God allowed it then, but today it would be an abomination. The mission of the first family was to multiply and replenish the world, and they did just that. They populated the earth. Somehow, the whole population had become wicked, and their imaginations were continually evil until God had repented that He ever created man. God concluded destroying the land, the people, and all the amenities. However, God's mercy said, "No, not all." But Noah found grace in the eyesight of God. He commanded him to build an ark, which had become a safe haven for Noah, his wife, his three sons, and their wives. They were the ones who replenished the earth anew.

Since that time, there is a male for a female vice versa. There is no need now for a man to marry his sister. Cain did it, Seth did it, it was okay for their circumstances, but it would be a disgrace today for you and me before the Lord. Just peek at Leviticus 20:17. Keep in mind, the euphemism of the flesh was a mess. When you allow the flesh to run wild without control, it is very perilous because the flesh is the primary tool of Satan. In King David's family, there was a shameful quarrel involving Absalom, Ammon, and their sister Tamar. Ammon allowed his flesh to fool him into committing the unconscionable act of raping his sister. When Ammon shared his desire to sleep with Tamar, she did not waste any time reminding him that she was his sister, and no such thing ought to be done in Israel. Ammon went with his folly, and when her brother Absalom found that out, he waited two years before killing his brother Ammon for raping their sister. (2 Samuel chapter 13)

CHAPTER FOUR

APPRECIATION THROUGH WORSHIP

Appreciation is a demonstration of worship. No one can sincerely worship God except they appreciate Him. When it is done this way, then worship becomes the outburst of a grateful and sincere heart willing to show appreciation and love to a merciful God. I would not mind using one of the patriarchs as an illustration, but why not use Noah, the father of our nation. After all, he introduced us to a great word that would become vital in the life of worship. The word is "ALTAR." Genesis chapter 8 and verse 20 said: "And Noah builded an altar unto the Lord; and took of every clean beast, and of every clean fowl, and offered burnt offerings on the altar." An altar is made for worship, and Noah here built one to show his appreciation to God after he and his family reached the dry land from the Ark. Note here, in his worship, he offered God the best from God's best. I use this term tp remind all of us that worship God in the ceremonial of giving. Be mindful, whatever we offer and give to God is God's in the first place, so let us give him our best. Noah demonstrated to us how worship was and is a personal affair between God and the worshipper. I do not recall a mandate from God that required Noah to offer burnt offerings to Him upon his arrival on dry land. It was a free-will offering to a well-deserved God. The offerings spoke for themselves because they displayed appreciation, honor, respect, love, and praise to an Almighty God. Remember that I mentioned earlier in a similar fashion that true worship could indeed soften God's heart and, through compassion, change God's mind. The sincerity of this offering had done both to God in Genesis chapter 8 and verse 21 and let us read: "And the Lord smelled a sweet savor; and the Lord said in His heart, I will not again curse the ground any more for man's sake; for the imagination of man's heart is evil from his youth; neither will I again smite any more everything living, as I have done." Thank God for this covenant. This was the result of a cheerful and free-will offering that was well pleased by God. We will never know how powerful our worship of God is until we are making it personal. It does not matter if the worship to God is done cooperatively or uncooperatively. It is still an individual thing. Keep in mind, we do not have the ability to know who is serious or not with

God, but individually speaking, we know if we are or are not serious with God. Do not think wrong of me; it is good to worship with others, but if there is a lack of truthfulness among the worshippers, just make sure that God can count on your worship. Be confident if you are a part of worship that God will always be satisfied regardless.

Worship, where was that word first recorded in the Bible? In Genesis chapter 22 and verse 5, "And Abraham said unto his young men, Abide ye here with the ass; and I and the lad will go yonder and worship, and come again to you."

Quite a verse in a fascinating chapter; it brings about so much controversy among theologians. I do not mind joining the group with an explanation in a little while, which is not based on opinion but fact.

The way the word worship was recorded in verse above proved clearly that the word was familiar to the young men who tagged along with Abraham and Isaac. However, the two young men were excluded from the worship by Abraham because it was a private and a family affair. Abraham had full knowledge of the term worship way before Moses penned his statement in the above verse. I do not know who introduced

Abraham to worship for a fact, even though I have a few opinions. However, there is the knowledge that I can take at face value. Abraham was the second recorded man beside Noah who built God an altar gratefully for appearing to him and giving him the command to leave his country, family, and father's house in exchange for a better land. (Genesis 12:1-7)

So far, we have learned from two patriarchs how to obey and appreciate God whenever He appears unto us for guidance, direction, protection, or anything else wherever we are; we need to convert the place to an altar and give God an appreciation and worship Him with these words "THANK YOU, LORD." Nowadays, with our knowledge, it is not hard to worship God whenever and wherever because we carry a portable altar. God has the key, and only God can hear us; this is our heart. It is a poor worshipper who never uses this altar to speak with God secretly. Remember, the heart is also the most effective form of communication with God. After Abraham received the Abrahamic covenant, guess what he did, he built another altar to worship God. When worship is truly in the system, it becomes quotidian and contagious to those around the worshiper. The biggest mistake we can make is to associate worship with the length of time.

A few seconds of prayer could have a greater effect on God than one, two, three hours of prayer or more depends on the circumstances. For example, I believe Apostle Peter had spent much time in the synagogue with Jesus where worship applied, but the night when he saw Jesus's walking on water and Jesus asked him to come according to his request. Peter came down from the ship, starting to walk on water toward Jesus. In doing so, Peter was distracted by the wind, he was also afraid, and he began to sink. Peter did not have time to say a long prayer because he was in trouble. All he had time to say was, "Lord, save me," and his Lord did. (Matthew 14:28-31)

I must give this illustration to eliminate any misuse of the statement made concerning "a few seconds of worship could have…" It is not an idea of worship for the Sabbath. When I was first introduced to worship, a few seconds in worship service suited me just fine, and the priest would not have any problem with me because I was playing worship to please my parents.

Let us fall right back on track with the 22nd chapter, where the word worship, per say, was first recorded. The Bible said if I might paraphrase the story "That God did tempt Abraham" by asking him to offer his lovely son Isaac as a burnt offering into the land of Moriah upon one of the mountains. (Verse 1, 2)

Before going any further, I need to quote a portion of verse 1, which becomes argumentative for looking for reasons to discredit our God. "And it came to pass after these things, that God did tempt Abraham," The word "Tempt" right here has been a distraction to those that choose to be distracted. They lost focus on the beauty of such a Verse because they think they have found evidence that supports their claims that the Bible is contradictory. They base their argument in James chapter 1 and verse 13 that says: "Let no man say when he is tempted, I am tempted of God: for God cannot be tempted with evil, neither tempteth He any man:" The conclusion to this matter is two different verses speaking about two other things and two different meanings of the word "Tempt." However, the message is the same if I am allowed to play with words. I am well acquainted with both theories, and I refuse to be distracted by senseless disputation. Our Spiritual life is nothing but a test. To see how much we love God. There are times in our lives when God has to step aside to test our faith and maturity in Him. God often allows the Holy Ghost to lead us to be tempted by the devil. We must go through as children of God this initiation process. Our devotional worship is what would strengthen us. Let us continue paraphrasing the 22nd chapter of Genesis.

God was introducing His folded plan of salvation for humankind to Abraham. Many might disagree with me, but God gave His Son to die on Calvary as a sacrifice for sins down the road.

Abraham, saddled his donkeys early in the morning and took two young men and Isaac, his son, with him as the story continues. On the third day, Abraham saw afar off the place for the sacrifice. (Verse 3, 4) There again was another folded glance at Calvary, and we know what took place on the third day, Jesus our Savior, God's Son, rose with all power in his hands.

Abraham promised the young men that he left behind a safe return for him and Isaac. He took the wood and gave it to Isaac to carry. Abraham carried the knife and the fire. Isaac called his father, and Abraham answered, here I am, son. And Isaac asked him a few questions that would indicate that the boy Isaac introduced to worship before, knew the precepts of burnt offering. Isaac said to his father, behold the fire and the wood, but where is the lamb? It need be for me to quote verse 7, 8 eight it is a must, "And Isaac spake unto Abraham his father, and said, my father; and he said, here am I, my son. And he said, Behold the fire and the wood: but where is the lamb for a burnt offering? And Abraham said, my son, God will provide Himself a lamb for a burnt offering: so they went both of them together."

In verse 5, was Abraham lied to the young men when promising he and Isaac safe returned knowing his intention?
In verse 8, was Abraham lying again to Isaac about the lamb?
Was Abraham lying to Isaac about God will provide Himself a Lamb?

Abraham never told them specifically that he and Isaac would both come back. However, he did tell them that they were going to worship. In my view, Abraham acted as though he was lying to Isaac. But when I look at the salvation story, Abraham was prophesying about our Savior Jesus the Christ throughout the journey. The way he answered Isaac's question was phenomenal. Honestly, that was an answer "flesh and blood did not reveal to him." Then, it came across as a lie to me, but now, I understand it better. It was pure prophesied. Abraham alone could not answer Isaac's question correctly, and no one from the Old

Testament could. It took John the Baptist to answer Isaac's question when he saw Jesus coming to baptize by him. He said, "Behold the Lamb of God, which taketh away the sin of the world." John 1: 29

The book of Revelation, chapter 5 and verse 12, puts the icing on the cake. "Saying with a loud voice, worthy is the Lamb that was slain to receive power, and riches, and wisdom, and strength, and honor, and glory, and blessing."

Abraham and Isaac arrived at the place where the sacrifice was supposed to be. He built an altar and followed the steps for a burnt offering. Abraham bound Isaac and laid him on the altar. He took the knife to slay him, and the angel of the Lord intervened on Isaac's behalf and stopped Abraham. Did Abraham pass the test? Yes, he did. As a result of his obedience, God promised to bless him.

Some theologians felt that Abraham was not honest. In other words, he was bluffing about slaying his son. He knew God would not allow him to do so. I am afraid I have to disagree with those comments. Again, we need not forget that God looks at the heart of men from time to time. In this case, if Abraham were not sincere about it and were only pretending that he was, therefore bypassing the angel of the Lord with the lie, we would need to re-evaluate the power of our God. There is one thing I know for sure no one can ever fool our God.

Abraham was as serious as serious could be. His readiness to offer the son that he loved substantially displayed his obedience and his love for God. However, Isaac's blood could have never been atonement for sin. However, it was not the end of the story. God did provide him a ram, and he offered it instead of Isaac as a sacrifice. Nonetheless, they did worship God.

It is a known fact that the God that we serve will not indulge in offering human sacrifices as a form of appreciation through worship for Him. If He does, it would be for teaching's sake. Shall we use, for example, the story of Jephthah the Gileadite in the book of Judges Chapter 11? We learned that he was a mighty man of valor. Gilead was his father, and his mother was a harlot. Jephthah had a few brothers from his father's side, and the brothers disowned him because his mother was a prostitute. Allow me to bring this point out, "The complex of superiority and inferiority is not that new. Spiritually speaking, the two complexes are the driving forces behind the division existing among so-called people of God in the house of God.

Jephthah's brothers classified him as inferior comparing to them because his mother was a strange woman. They refused to accept him for who he was. Their moral values could not cope with their brother's mother's lifestyle. What did that have to do with Jephthah? They felt he was born in sin, but what about them. Therefore, Jephthah was not fit to be their brother. These attitudes should not take anyone by surprise in the Spiritual realm if the truth is told. Too often, we refuse to accept people for who they are because we often forget that God is the one that does the changing in people's lives, not we. Keep in mind here that Jephthah and Jesus our Savior had something in common. Jephthah's mother was a harlot, and Jesus' great grandmother, Rehab, was her name. She, too was a harlot. (Matthew 1: 5) Thank God for the scriptures, and why not move on. Jephthah's brothers had decided to run him out of the country through expulsion. He fled from his brothers, and tagging along with him was some worthless men. The elders of Gilead were about to live the concept, "But many that are first shall be last; and the last shall be first." Matthew 19 verse 30.

The children of Ammon invaded Israel, and the panic of the war had a stronghold on Israel. Then Jephthah's brothers took a memorable trip to the land of Tob to make a proposition to Jephthah. They wanted him to be their captain so they could fight the children of Ammon. Here again, a perfect demonstration of scripture which primarily said in Psalm 118 verse 22 "The stone which the builders refused is become the head stone of the corner."

I am required to quote Jephthah's answer to his brothers in verse 7 of the 11th chapter of the book of Judges because it is beautiful. Like my mother often said, "God has a way that is mighty sweet but bitter to the devil." Here is the quote, "And Jephthah said to the elders of Gilead, Did not ye hate me, and expel me out of my father's house? And why are ye come unto me now when ye are in distress?" Beautiful! Isn't it?

Jephthah made it clear to them if God delivered the children of Ammon in his hands, would he be chief over them? Without hesitation, they agreed with the condition, and they made God the witness of the covenant between Jephthah and them. The elders stood by their words; upon Jephthah's arrival in his native land, the people made Jephthah the son of the harlot head and captain over them. He sent a messenger to the king to see how the war could be avoided. The king presented his demand by the same messenger, which was the repossession of their land from Israel, the only option that would end the war. That option, instead of coming to a compromise it rather turned Jephthah into a temporary preacher. He preached to the king through the messenger. The sermon did not affect the king at all.

As you know, the Spirit of the Lord in the Old Testament time was to empower believers for a short term. That was one of his missions. He comes and goes. Now the Bible says, "The Spirit of the Lord came upon Jephthah and he passed over Gilead, Manasseh, and passed over Mizpeh of Gilead and from Mizpeh of Gilead he passed over unto the children of Ammon," Judges 11 and verse29. Jephthah is about to do something unthinkable. He made a questionable vow to God, which made me wonder what possessed him to do that way.

There is nothing wrong with making a vow to God. It is a beautiful thing, especially when standing by it. A vow made to God is a promise made to God. We have been warned that it is better not to make a vow to God than make one and break it. The Preacher in the book of Ecclesiastes put it in a more eloquent way than I do, and he said, "When thou vowest a vow unto God, defer not to pay it; for He hath no pleasure in fools: pay that which thou hast vowed.

Better is it thou shouldest not vow, than that shouldest vow and not pay." Ecclesiastes 5:4, 5 Keep in mind that making promises to God is a voluntary thing, and God is the last person to lie to because He does not care too much for a liar. Some of us, as worshippers of God, do not fully understand the vow or the promise.

We can vows to God privately or publicly. Secretly is between God and me. Publicly, Lord have mercy, is between me, and God, and His people. When a worshipper keeps breaking vows, he makes them publicly; his credibility diminishes rapidly. For example, if I stood in a Sunday school class and said, "I promise the Lord starting today I will be in Sunday school every Sunday, and after that, I come for two Sundays, and then I stopped coming; I automatically become a liar and a covenant breaker. If I kept lying before God and His people like that on other issues to receive some emotional Amen, God could turn me over to a reprobate mind. At this point, can God count on me? "What do you think?"

Our most significant issues are, we enjoyed blowing the trumpet to make public our vows to God: for example, listen to this so-called testimony, "Church I told the Lord if He gave me a job, I would pay my tithes, or I would faithfully worship Him," and then the Lord answers the prayer. A testifier gives a testimony, and the church claps their hands, does a holy dance with multiple Amens and that was the last time they saw the person. As the old saying says, "liar, liar pants on fire." Again, the book of Ecclesiastes 5:2 – 3 "Be not rash with thou mouth, and let not thine heart be hasty to utter anything before God: for God is in heaven, and thou upon earth: therefore, let thy words be few. For a dream cometh through the multitude of business; and a fool's voice is known by multitude of words."

Voluntarily, Jephthah decided to make a vow to God. Let us look at the nature of the vow in Judges 11 verse 30, 31, "And Jephthah vowed a vow unto the Lord, and said, if thou shalt without fail deliver the children of Ammon into mine hands, Then it shall be, that whatsoever cometh forth of the doors of my house to meet me, when I return in peace from the children of Ammon, shall surely be the Lord's, and I will offer it up for a burnt offering."

Quite a vow, he promised to show his appreciation through worship to God. He even specified the type of burnt offering and how he expected to find it if he returned in peace. Well, God delivered what he asked for without a problem. Jephthah won the war. At this point, not even Jephthah knew what he was going to sacrifice for the Lord. All he knew thus far was that there would be a burnt offering appreciation service for the Lord according to his vow. In verses 34, 35, we learned, "And Jephthah came to Mizpeh unto his house, and, behold, his daughter came out to meet him with timbrels and with dances: and she was his only child; beside her he had neither son nor daughter. And it came to pass when he saw her, that he rent his clothes, and said, alas, my daughter! Thou hast brought me very low, and thou art one of them that trouble me: for I have opened my mouth unto the Lord, and I cannot go back."

Jephthah's story was a breathtaking one that caused many questions to cross my intellect. Was Jephthah customized in human sacrifices? Was Jephthah expecting an animal or someone else to come out and meet him? Did God allow him to go through with the burnt offering? Was Jephthah a God-fearing man? I could express my opinion of Jephthah's vow to God and the way he went about it. There was no doubt about his sincerity, but he should have been more precise about what he wanted to offer as a burnt offering to God.

Furthermore, in making the vow, Jephthah never dreamed that his only daughter would be the one out of the house first. If he had known that, I believe he would have gone another route. I could imagine the look on Jephthah's face when he saw his daughter, but his action explained it all when he rent his clothes. We do need to consider a few things when he said, "whatsoever cometh forth of the doors of my house;" The statement covered both human beings and domesticating animals which was familiar with the sound of victory often went out to meet their masters to be part of the celebration. He did not say, "Neither Whosoever nor whoever but "whatsoever" came out of his house to meet him. He said, "I will offer it for a burnt offering. Keep in mind that Jephthah said, "I will offer it." He did not say a person. To me, that refuted the idea that he was gearing up for human sacrifices. If that statement had any truth to it, Jephthah learned a great lesson from it. One thing I know, worship God through ignorance can be costly.

In my opinion, Jephthah was well acquainted with human sacrifices, but that day I believe he had animals in mind for the burnt offering instead of his daughter. In this situation, God had nothing to do with Jephthah's decision to offer a victory sacrifice through a burnt offering if God made him victorious. God delivered, and he expected Jephthah to do accordingly regardless. Remember, by reading the story from the beginning to the end, and we could conclude that Jephthah was a strong-minded man who had great respect for the law of God. His faith in God would not allow him to change his mind about sacrificing his only daughter. The fact of the matter was she came out first from the house. Everything I just said is debatable because I am thinking again, but I believe we can agree that Jephthah and his daughter both knew how solemn a vow made to God could be. In the book of Numbers, Chapter 30 and verse 2 says, "If a man vow a vow unto the Lord, or swear an oath to bind his soul with a bond; he shall not break his word, he shall do according to all that proceeded out of his mouth."

I have great respect for Jephthah's daughter, who courageously accepted the lot that was falling on her. The comments she made to her father indicated that his decision was well with her soul. Even though it encircled her mind with sadness, she even reminded her father, in a way, of the importance of keeping a vow, vowed to God. She said that if he opened his mouth unto the Lord, he had to do to her according to what he promised God he would do. Strange that she knew what the deal was without him going through the full details. However, she requested two things from her father. "Two months alone to go up and down upon the mountains to bewail her virginity with the fellows," before her execution.

Making a constructive vow to God is one ingredient that make worship more enjoyable, lovable, and honorable. One of the purposes of worship is to help the soul prosper, as it reaches maturity in God. Understand, worship boosts our love for God, and it teaches us how to be serious with Him in our vows. There is one other thing I observe about Abraham and Jephthah their faith can be trusted. Remember a faith, which had not been tested, could not be counted. We can agree that both of them had been put to the test and graduated with honors.

In my conclusion, did God accept Jephthah's daughter as a burnt offering? In my opinion, the answer is no. I believe God rejected Jephthah's offering as He did Cain's and others.

Why did God stop Abraham from sacrificing Isaac? And did not stop Jephthah from doing the same thing to his daughter?

Do not forget that Abraham's readiness to offer Isaac was merely a freewill offering; it was a recommendation from God. Therefore, God would be responsible for the outcome either way, but He chose to stop it. However, Jephthah's vow to offer a burnt offering was voluntary without any subjection at all from God. Therefore, it was up to Jephthah to be a man of his words or a liar. After all God did deliver.

No one knows the conclusion if he sacrificed his daughter or not, even though I believe that he did.

Let me pray before continuing, Dear Lord, I thank You for Your words, and I ask You to keep on teaching me the artful of worship so the vows that I vow to You would not be through ignorance, but through maturity of faith, Amen.

CHAPTER FIVE

WORSHIP KILLERS

Worshipping God in is very powerful along with praise, which is its glamour and always brings positive results. Worship is not optional but essential to those seeking a closer and serious relationship with God, relationships based on faithfulness. Worship is our survival kit. It is our passport and ticket for those of us who are citizens of heaven. It is the heartbeat of our Spiritual lives. However, worship is not immortal, but it could be all lies in the worshipper's hands. The thing that I love most about the art of worship is the power that every believer has in their hands to develop a powerful worship lifestyle. This ability may not appear overnight, but the steps toward this goal require love, devotion, dedication, determination, perseverance, adoration, and faithfulness. We need them to remain stable and devout in the worship of God. Otherwise, the chance to survive Satan's attack would be slimmed.

Earlier on, if I am not mistaken, I remembered sharing that worship is mostly all about attitudes. Therefore, we need to be ready to worship whenever and wherever God summons us for this purpose. Remember, worship could be spontaneous, especially when found favor with God. Moses, the author of the Pentateuch, was well acquainted with the spontaneity of prayer. Moses was minding his business when the angel of the Lord appeared to him in a flame of fire in the middle of a bush. His curiosity went wild because the fire did not consume the bush. He decided to turn aside to investigate the wonder of the burning bush. God saw how puzzled Moses was; He called him twice by his name from the midst of the burning bush.

Moses intelligently answered, "Here am I." God commanded him to remove his shoes because the ground where he stood was Holy. God introduced Himself to Moses, and He commissioned him to go and deliver the children of Israel. (Exodus 3: 2-10)

Moses's encounter with God in the burning bush gave indisputable proof of God's omnipresent attribute and how private and confidential worship and praise was and are. Even when it occurs publicly, it is still an intimate and personal matter. It does not matter how many people assembled in one place worshipping God. That does not change the nature of worship and praise. Its status remains private and personal because prayer and praise are constantly dealing with the sincerity of the heart of the individual worshipper among a group of worshippers. In worship and praise, the outward of worshippers could be very deceptive to its peers because of the status of limitation as far as the heart is concerned.

We cannot see what is in the man's heart unless it divinely reveals, but God knows the inward of all worshipper's fake or real because He observes the hearts. God could have sent Moses' father-in-law or Aaron, his brother, to deliver the children of Israel. No, He selected Moses through a heart-searching process. This procedure of God or this selection method is an ongoing process until the Day of the Lord when all the saints of God will elevate from Sanctification, Justification, and Glorification. I often think about this Great Day.

A few days before Easter in 2013, I was in the process of fulfilling my Lent obligation toward our God. The Spirit of our Lord compels me to imagine the event of the Day of Redemption.

When all the saints of God procession in before the Throne. I was sitting in my car in a grocery store parking lot waiting for my beautiful wife Joy, who promise to go inside the store and grab a few things. I was ready to tag along with her. Then, she turned around as if she received a command from God for me to wait in the car. With a sweet voice, she said, "Honey, you do not have to come. It will only take a few minutes to pick up what I need. I will be right back." She spoke like the store was hers. The idea of waiting in line to pay for her merchandise did not seem to cross her mind. My wife is a truthful person, but her five minutes could quickly become two hours for her shopping moments. So, I pulled my seat back and got ready for a nap. Earlier that morning, in one of my worship moments during the day, I remembered asking God for a brand new song besides all the twenty-some plus Spiritual worship and praise songs he gave me already to sing for Him on Easter Sunday Morning Service. The five minutes had long gone, and my eyes chased away the nap, but I trained myself whenever the discomfort of sleep invaded my being; instead of remaining restless through the day or the night, I immediately consecrated myself unto worship. Right there in my car, I spontaneously began to worship and praise our God personally and personally. Right there in my car, the parking lot had automatically become "Holy Ground" because, at this point, I was in the presence of God. I will highlight this phrase because I need to return to it after telling the story to show a missed identification.

In that same hour, God had given me the song entitled "ON THAT DAY," and I quickly wrote these words of the song, which may not make any sense to others, and He gave me the lyrics. Let me bother you with it for a minute, and it goes like this:

On Your Way to Glory
You showed your love for me.
Alone I was afraid to be.
In the darkness, I was afraid to walk.
Somehow, you looked beyond my fault,
Left me the Holy Ghost
To abide in me forever.
He will lead me and guide me.
Until the Day of the Lord.
He will lead me and guide me/
Until the day of redemption.
On that Day, I must be there
To see when God Himself
Crown You, Jesus King of Kings.
On that Day, I must be there
To see when God Himself
Crown You, Lord of Lords.
On that Day, I must be there
To hear the choir sings
Worthy is the Lamb.

Worthy is the Lamb
That was slain on Calvary.
Right there before the Angels
Jesus got up and rose again
With all power in His hands.
Jesus got up for you and me.

It is a beautiful song. When my wife got back into the car, she had a buggy filled with merchandise. She told me; she did not know what kept her so long inside the store. I gave her a refreshing smile to indicate I knew why. It was God's doing because He searched my heart and decided it was the right time for me to write and learn the song.

The funny thing about me writing Spiritual songs and singing them privately and publicly is that I do not have an attractive voice that could please man's ears. The consciousness of that belief was enough to kill my worship, and praise like it did before. I love to sing unto the Lord because He is the only one, I believe, who truly enjoys my singing. How do I know that? He keeps on giving me all these songs to write, and no one ever comes to claim them from me. My wife Joy sings pretty well. She has a voice that can captivate the ears of an audience. She often jokes and says she would not have married me if she had heard me singing before she dated me. This is how bad my singing voice sounds to her. Joy had a wonderful testimony. She said, "She loves singing also. One day she was making what I called a husband checklist before God. She asked God for a husband that would treat her like a queen. One that fears God, as the list goes on. She messed around asking God for a man who loves to sing. What she meant was a man that knew how to sing so they could make beautiful harmony together. However, she omitted that part from her husband's checklist. She only said a man that loves to sing. Well, God graciously gave her the desire of her heart, including a man who loved to sing, but not one that could make harmony with her to attract man's ears. He gave her one who loved to make harmony unto God's ears. Joy loves me, and she is my number one fan except for the singing. But guess what? She is singing those songs with me in worship service, unaware that we are making harmony together for the Lord. My wife is the closest person to me, and for this reason, she could help kill my worship in the song, however unintentional. She was expressing her true feelings about my singing in her joking. However, at the end of the day, it is left up to me to shy away from singing worship and praise songs amid an assembly or to keep on lifting His Name in songs. As a result, my love for singing to God has increased tremendously. Even in my preaching and teaching of the gospel in English, my French accent could have been burdensome to me, especially when someone hears me for the first time and says, "I did not understand a word you said, but I loved your accent. I love the way you speak." Others came and said, "I enjoyed the word. I heard every single word of it." I often answered these types of comments saying, "To God is the Glory."

Both statements were distracting enough to make me lose focus and kill my worship for a season. They had succeeded because it became all about me instead of God. Come to think of it, these worshippers did not mean any harm. They were only expressing their feeling. Let me rephrase that quick, some of them did not mean any harm, but some did. Ineffectively they were trying hard to give me a one-way ticket to the land of giving up and quit.

The minute I allow maturity in God to take its course through effective worship into my life, I resurrect my worship and praise through fasting, prayer, reading the holy word, and singing worship and praise songs. I put it like this because there is a difference between worship songs and praise songs. It would have been a crime against knowledge to equalize both after knowing the difference between the two. Worship songs do learn how to soften and melt God's heart. It covers a broad territory in a believers' life. Keep in mind worship, and praise to God is not about singing only. I can worship God without singing a song and praise Him without singing also.

However, singing songs to make melody unto God plays a significant role in worship and praise. For example, if prayer and knowing the word is the Super Star of prayer and praise, the co-star has to be and must be singing, vice versa. Worship songs open the door of humility. It is an invitation to God to search the heart, prove to Him how much we love Him and how badly we want Him to cover us with assurance under His guaranteed insurance, eternal life, and safekeeping on earth. Praise songs often brag on God for His marvelous works in creation as the only Architect, a Promise Keeper, a Savior, a Deliverer, a Victory Giver, a Problem Solver. The lyrics of a song are what determines the classification of the music as worship or praise songs. To be honest, some praise songs could serve as distractions to the actual worship to the point of killing the worship because they were singing at the wrong time. Once upon a time in my life, I was going through a situation that surprised me, but the case could not have happened any better time than when it occurred because I was amid forty nights of services to commemorate the entry of a New Year.

Everyone in my circle knew about the problem that I was facing. Some prayed honestly for me, and some hoped to see the end of my Spiritual era and watch me fall hard on my face. Some of my friends, God bless their hearts, were very sincere in the advice they gave me. Every single night, they prayed for me. They sang both types of songs, worship and praise on my behalf to the Lord. Still, the severity of the matter was increasing instead of diminishing. Deep down inside, I felt that worship in an orderly fashion was the only thing that could bring me out regardless of the beautiful advice given to me by friends and family. I had a strong feeling that worship was a solemn solution to my problem. One night, God gave me a worship song in a dream. I awoke and wrote the lyrics. He showed me how to prepare the temple for orderly worship. I knew then that God had introduced me to another form of worship that would be hard for other worshippers to digest because it was contrary to their traditional ways of worship. I had to choose whom to please between God and friends. That evening, after the dream, I went to the store and purchased the command ingredients, and I prepared the church for this orderly worship. When I began the service, I found myself singing that worship song entitled, "On my knees," and I started:

Here I am on my knees,
Patiently, waiting to hear a word from you.
Jesus, you know a word from you is all I greatly need.
Here I am in your presence, weeping, crying, and worshipping you.
Jesus, you know that your worship is bread for a life like mine.
Here I am as a sinner, saved by grace, waiting to be used by you.
Jesus, you know that I am your servant; use me as you please.
Here I am on my knees, patiently waiting for a miracle.
Jesus, you know your miracle is what is keeping me alive.
Here I am in your presence calling upon your Holy Name,
Jesus, you know your holy name is what I want to hear.

Right after singing that worship song, I felt my burdens lifted. Among the worshippers that gathered, I was declared victorious on the spot by a Messenger of

God whose name was not revealed to me. While the Messenger was leaving the Sanctuary, he made his presence known to the ushers who stood in front of the doors by allowing them to open up widely by themselves. We did have a Christophony experience. When I got up from my knees and shared my incredible experience to the Church how a Messenger from God came and gave me the victory, now he gave me a song of praise to write as the victory seal. The two ushers shared their experience at the door that night. One of the deacons shared how he saw somebody stand over me. Again, amid the worshippers, some tried to kill these worship experiences by saying the doors opened because it was very windy outside. They did not see any messenger pass by them. They left that night believing those of us who experienced the encounters classified as delusional. As true worshippers of God, our job is not to pressure others to accept our deposition. Otherwise, we leave ourselves open to be victims of distraction. Being distracted Spiritually could fully infect our blessings with unbelief and our growth in the Lord.

For some reason, when I was going through my dilemma, I never blamed the devil for my shortcoming because I always believe what I was going through was a preparation for more remarkable ministry. However, the song of praise that the Messenger gave me to write as my victory seal had a lot to do with Satan. When I considered the song's lyrics, it appeared that Satan's desire to sift me like wheat was enormous. Through the dictation of the Messenger, I wrote the song entitled "Satan, you can't touch me. " It goes like this:

There I was, deep down in the pit.
There I was crying; Lord have mercy.
Satan had me bound; Satan had me captive,
In a pit filled with sins, filled with sins.
I cried Dear Jesus; I repented to all my sins.
Come to my rescue, and He came, forgave all my sins.
And He renewed my mind, body, and soul.
And told Satan, Satan you can't touch this.
You tried Pierre, (Job, Abraham, Daniel,) and you failed,
Satan, you can't touch this.
You can't touch what is in God's hands.
Satan, you can't touch this.
You can't curse whom God bless. Satan you can't touch this.

This is a praise song and not a worship song. Some of you, in all sincerity, might warn me of the song because it is challenging Satan's ego. Sarcastically, I am afraid, and I am scared! Worshippers of God, please remember Satan is extremely passionate about the desire to harm us. The word desire means to want something strongly. Satan is loaded with desires. Let me make you shout, "Glory Alleluia," but you and I know the God who could allow or renounce the fulfillment of Satan's desires. Satan is a powerful creature, but who can stop us besides ourselves from being powerful worshippers of God, no one.

Do you remember this phrase right here? I promise to show a misidentification on my part when I said: The car and the parking lot had automatically become "Holy Ground" because, at this point, I was in the presence of God.

Who can steal or deprive us of our identity of who we indeed are in the Lord? It could be Satan, family members, friends, acquaintances, total strangers, and material things. I disagree totally because self and self alone steals and deprives us of our own identity in God through a process called low Spiritual self-esteem.

The misidentification on my part is that I should have known wherever I am and wherever you are; it does not matter, we are always in the presence of God, and it is subject to worship. For example, to say hello to someone you meet in a supermarket or in the street and you two started to talk about God spontaneously, the act of worship and praise has begun. Your presence will have already prepared the place for worship. I am trying to say that wherever and whenever we enter in a place spiritually speaking, we are never alone because Goodness and Mercy always come with us and boosts our readiness to worship. I do not know why we keep forgetting one of the most lavish promises He ever made to us before His departure from earth to Glory. He will be with us always.

Worship and praise are what identifies us with God. It is what makes us a particular people and a royal priesthood. We have an obligation to keep our worship in perfect shape free from distraction and drama caused by worship killers. Whom do I call worship killers? Am I talking about the devil, family members, friends, acquaintance, and materialistic things? Yes, so we thought. In a serious manner, who could actually kill my worship? Let me answer the first question worship killer could be the worshipper himself if he allowed his worship to be hindered. What about the second questions? Those mentioned could serve as a volunteer or as a volunteer coach to the worshipper; however, the worshipper is mainly responsible for killing his worship through distraction of others. Now let us follow some examples from the greatest and most important world most extensive library in the world, which is the "BIBLE." Let us go straight ahead from the book of 1 Samuel Chapter 1 to see a rival and a priest trying to cause a believer by the name of Hannah to hinder her own worship. The rival provoked Hannah sorely and the priest accused her of disorderly conduct by defaming her character. Let me elaborate on the beginning of the story. There was a man name Elkanah who had two wives.

Please remember that polygamy, which translated from the Greek polygamy/polygamous, was acceptable at that time. A man was allowed to have more than one wife because the commandment that God gave to man was still in effect, "Be fruitful and multiply the land." Besides, there was a shortage of males since when Moses was born. The king had passed an ordinance to kill all males children born and the idea had brought a shortage of men to that era. (Exodus 4)

Elkanah had two wives Hannah and Penninah, who had a tremendous advantage on Hannah because she did have children for Elkanah, but Hannah had no children. Elkanah every year went to Shilow to worship and to sacrifice, in other words, to bring something valuable unto the Lord. The word sacrifice derives from the Latin word "Sacrificium," meaning "Making sacred." Yearly he went up to do just that. However, why worship God yearly? The Old Testament saints did not fully understand the requirements of worship. However, that little bit of knowledge they had was good enough to please God. They felt that the mountain of Jerusalem was the number one place to worship and bring the sacrifice of praise to God. Worship through ignorance again is always acceptable to God until knowing better. Yearly worship would not work for any worshipper of God who knew the rope in this day and age. However, we find some today worship Him once a week on Sunday, only following the grandfather's special day to worship. However, maturity teaches that our worship is so essential until it requires twenty-four hours a day from our time. Do you now see how vital worship is in the life of a worshipper? Worship is a mind and a heart thing, which makes you a constant and stable worshipper. I have a terrible case of side-tracking whenever I talk about worshipping God. Let us go back to the story. When the time had presented itself for offerings, Elkanah, gave to his wife Penninah and her children a portion of the offerings in the presence of the priests. Then he offered Hannah worthy amounts because he loved her the most. However, Hannah had a serious problem that could hinder her worship, and what was that? God had shut up her womb. She was incapable of giving birth to a child. In the society Hannah was living in, it was a disgrace as well as shameful when a woman could not produce a child for her husband. Penninah, Hannah's rival, did not feel Hannah's pain and sorrow at all. Instead of Penninah sympathizing with Hannah, she rather rejoiced in Hannah's dilemma by making her feel less than a woman. We see how cold some worshippers can be. Do not forget, and there are two ways man worship God, in the TRUTH and a LIE. In this aspect, only God knows who is who. We need to look at a few verses in this Chapter to understand the mean side of Penninah and the judgmental mind of Eli, who had been introduced to a new way of worship by Hannah.

The power of a praying woman through worship, look how Hannah's rival Penninah involuntarily leads Hannah to the blessings of her life. Let us start with verse 6 of 1Samuel Chapter 1 because I already gave the scope from verse 1- 5, and her adversary also provoked her sore, for to make her fret because God had shut up her womb.

Peninnah irritated and made fun of Hannah a great deal until she took away her appetite and turned Hannah's eyes unto a fountain of tears, right in the midst of the worship service. Penninah was enjoying Hannah's misfortune instead of worshipping God on Hannah's behalf for her deliverance. Peninnah's Spirit still exists among believers today. In most worship services, we would find some who have been judged, criticized, laughed at, picked on, and talked about right there in the presence of God during His worship service. Bold are those who have that Peninnah's Spirit, and they do not have a fear of God because of a lack of knowledge and wisdom.

Hannah's melancholic and tearful moment reached the heart of her husband, who tried to remind her how good he had been to her better than everybody else. The Bible says that Hannah excused herself after everyone ate and drank in Shiloh. Eli, the priest, took a seat by the post of the temple of the Lord. Hannah was in bitterness of soul, and prayed unto the Lord, and wept sore. (Verse 8-10) In the following verse, Hannah decided to do something, in my opinion, she had not done in years past. She took her complaint to God. She finally realized the best way to communicate with God and whatever she needed from God was through worship. Maturity had made its appearance in her life. Who knew in the years passed that Hannah could have followed Peninnah's nonsense to the tenth power by giving her a "piece of her mind?" She had obeyed what I called one of the laws of a worshipper, remain focus and tell God all about it.

My experience in this journey requires me to believe that focusing is the remedy to distraction which, keeps us far away from God's blessings.

What did Hannah say to God? Quote, "And she vowed a vow, and said, O Lord of hosts, if thou wilt indeed took on the affliction of thine handmaid, and remember me, and not forget thine handmaid, but wilt give unto thine handmaid a man child, then I will give him unto the Lord all the days of his life, and they shall no razor come upon his head. And it came to pass, as she continued praying before the Lord, that Eli marked her mouth." Verse 11 and 12

Quite a penitential prayer coming from Hannah's heart, it was encircled with sincerity. Again, worship is indeed a personal affair between God and His child. However, some people may feel she was bargaining with God. If true, what difference did that make? It was between her and God. She vowed a vow that pleased God's ears and melted His Heart. In verse 13, we learned, "Now Hannah, she spake in her heart; only her lips moved, but her voice was not heard: therefore Eli thought she had been drunken."

Eli, the priest, was accustomed to hearing worshippers pray aloud; even when they turned it down on a low key, He was able to read their lips. This time he was unable to read Hannah's lips. Negatively, he concluded that she was drunk instead of allowing her room to finish her frank talk with God. This worship was private, and Eli served as an intruder to disturb Hannah's focused heart. Who knows, maybe Hannah had a drinking problem in the past, which triggered the priest to insinuate she was drunk. It could be that he had never seen Hannah behave like this before. He was accustomed to a Hannah who took worship as a hobby. This Hannah in question was worshipping her God with a purpose in her heart. Here I am about to re-enter another controversial statement, no believers in God should worship and praise Him without a goal, whether it is done quotidian; worship and praise should never be performed as a hobby, but as a duty to God. Because of their dominant characteristic, worship and praise can easily be performed as a hobby by immature worshippers instead of with purpose. Worship and praise cannot help themselves from being the center of God's movement. It is difficult, almost impossible, to teach Bible study, talk about the affairs of God impart of worship and praise, again purpose strongly recommended by God Himself.

Verse 14, "And Eli said unto her, How long wilt thou be drunken? Put away thy wine from thee."

The priest, in this situation, appeared he was not in tune with God. Otherwise, it would have been revealed divinely to him to leave her alone.

Aggressive criticism along with perjury toward a struggling believer in the house of God could drive them into a backslidden state. It is imperative to share with others not to let this type of thing defer and delay their growth because, amid of persecution, there is deliverance and vengeance for those that can stand the harassment.

In verses 15 - 17 said, "And Hannah answered and said, No, my Lord, I am a woman of a sorrowful Spirit: I have drunk neither wine nor strong drink, but have poured out my soul before the Lord. Count not thine handmaid for a daughter of Belial: for out of the abundance of my complaint and grief have I spoken hitherto. Then Eli answered and said, go in peace and the God of Israel grant thee thy petition that thou hast asked of him."

Let us take into consideration what I said above concerning Eli, the priest. This might sound like double talk for the sake of knowledge and Hannah and her plight. Was Eli wrong for thinking Hannah was drunk? Did Hannah utterly understand why Eli thought she was drunk? Did Hannah have control over her behavior? Did Eli believe her story? The answers to those questions may surprise many but remember, the law of agreeing or disagree is still enforced. Directly, Eli was not wrong for thinking Hannah was drunk. He was intensely passionate and serious in the affairs of God that were what activated his readiness to rebuke her severely. He based his judgment on her behavior. He was in the dark about the concealment of the Holy Ghost or Spirit. And His effect on those who received Him. If the Holy Ghost or Spirit were revealed at that time, Eli would understand Hannah's behavior. Hannah herself was in the same boat as Eli as far as this knowledge was concerned. Whenever a worshipper worships God in the Spirit as Hannah did, the Holy Ghost or Spirit has no other choice but to overshadow the worshipper. The Holy Ghost or Spirit, with your permission, is whom I call the Seal approval of God. If

God is pleased with the worship and praise, believe me, the Spirit would be automatically the center of the worship service.

Hannah remained in the dark of Eli's reason for believing she was drunk. She did not waste any time defending her character. I think that day when Eli left his post to come closer to her, with his nose, he gave Hannah a breathalyzer test. She passed the test because there was no smell of wine and strong drink in her breath.

Speaking from experience, the Holy Ghost or Spirit in a worshipper could send mixed signals to those who have never been in contact with Him through His manifestation. They could easily associate Him with new wine or strong drink.

Hannah could not help herself in the way she was behaving. She and Eli were ignorant of the Comforter. Look what happened on the day of Pentecost. The day that changed the phase of worship forever was the day that unsealed the concealment of the Third Person of the Trinity, "The Holy Ghost or Spirit." The mission of the Spirit was revealed for the good of our understanding. The story started by introducing us to the two most powerful words in worship, Acts Chapter 2 verse 1, "And when the day of

Pentecost was fully come, they were all with one accord in one place."

"One Accord" is the two most powerful and important words in the cooperation of worship. Do I need to pray before making the following statement because I do not want to offend anyone? Here comes the statement, The Holy Ghost or Spirit would not have come that day if the disciples were not in "ONE ACCORD." Remember, there was a division among the disciples, and Judas Iscariot was the one who caused all the turmoil. His seat was still vacant. Therefore, the house was not in order to receive such a Holy Being. In Acts Chapter 1, verse 23, we see where the eleven got together in a worship service to fill the vacant seat. They appointed two men, Joseph, and Matthias. They did something very splendid before selecting the next apostle. They did not choose him because he could sing and preach or because he was nice-looking or knew influential people in the assembly. Look what they did in verse 24, "And they prayed, and said, Thou, Lord, which knowest the hearts of all men, shew whether of these two thou hast chosen," Verse 25, 26 said, "That he may take part of this ministry and apostleship, from which Judas by transgression fell, that he might go to his own place. And they gave forth their lots; and the lot fell upon Matthias; and he was numbered with the eleven apostles."

Let us whisper a prayer before I continue. Father God, we thank You for this worship moment that You allowed us to have with You right now. Lord, please take control over our lives and our decision-making to better serve your people without partiality. In Jesus' Name, we pray, Amen.

Before the Holy Ghost made His entry into the place, the Bible says, "There was a sound from heaven as a mighty rushing wind and filled the house where they were sitting, and cloven tongues as of fire appeared and sat on each one of them." (Acts 2:2 and 3)

This is what I call fire baptism, and this baptism is an ordinance as well as an initiation to all worshippers who are in good standing with God.

After the disciples experienced the triumphal entry of the Holy Ghost, who came to reside on earth with us, the Bible said they were filled with the Holy Ghost and began to speak in other tongues, as the Spirit gave them utterance to express themselves in essential speech. The Holy Ghost made sure men of every nation under the blue sky heard the noise. They came together confounded, shocked that they were able to understand each other language clearly without translators. That day, universal worship and praise to a universal language of people was the highlight of the day. He tore up the barrier of languages until every man realized this was the wonderful work of God. That day, as far as worship is concerned, "the rain had fallen on the just and unjust." In doing this, the Holy Ghost had brought us back from the story of the Tower of Babel when there was one universal language upon the earth, but God had to confuse their language to slow down their evilness.

Verse 12 and 13 of the 2nd Chapter of the book of Acts is what reminded me of Hannah and Eli, who thought she was drunk, "And they were all amazed, and were in doubt, saying one to another, what meaneth this? Others mocking said, these men are full of new wine."

How sad ignorance could be. Here the doors of opportunity were wide open for them to join the great family of God in worship. However, the condition of their heart denied them this privilege. The blessings were available, and they forfeited them because they were too busy criticizing God's people in the manner they were worshipping. People now and then have not changed that much, but God is the same "yesterday, today, and tomorrow."

The conclusion of Hannah's worship experience had shown that whatever a worshipper yearned for could be obtained in his worship. Hannah's determination and dedication gave her the victory. God blessed her with a son named Samuel, and she turned him over to the service of God. She kept the vow she made unto God. Therefore, Hannah earnestly owned the trust of God. She kept her worship alive regardless of the obstacles she met in the middle of it.

The following person in the Bible that I genuinely admire is Job because of the sincerity of his worship and praise. He was confronted with many obstacles after Satan attacked his body. There are four people whom Job should have counted on for support alas, they had become his distraction, advisers, and accusers. One of them was his wife. She lost her cool when she saw how sick her husband was. She could not cope with his belief in how he held fast to his integrity through worship and praise to God. Job turned his sickness into a ministry minister and preached to a wrongly concerned wife and three self-righteous friends. Job's entourage was people who should have called a worship and praise service on his behalf for a miracle of healing. Eliphaz, Bildad, and Zophar made an appointment, and they did come to mourn with Job and comfort him (Job 2:11). Oh no, they were too hostile toward Job even to turn things positive. The three friends were more ready to investigate Job's sins as if they were sinless themselves. They associated his sickness with sins he had committed against God; little did they know, Job's sickness was a preparation for a much better and prosperous life ahead.

I cannot express enough in the ears of God's people that it does not matter how silly it may sound. The meaning of worship to me is to tend to your own business for God. Do not worry about other people's relationship with God until you know that yours could be displayed spiritually and sincerely as an example for others to follow. If we ever encounter a situation where sickness, misfortune, and hardship invade someone's life our Christian duty is to pray for them. In other words, minister to their needs through worship and praise. Leave all the "Why's" for God to handle because their hardship could be a test of faith for them and us. Keep in mind our worship is in vain until repentance after opinionating strongly, maliciously, and harshly against a worshipper that we worship with often.

Let us visit Job's wife's statement. A statement she released in frustration and pity for her sick husband. She knew he did not deserve that. She felt Job's integrity was what kept him alive. Still, she did not act on her belief because if his integrity could prevent him from dying, it could also heal him. How do I know she felt that way? In Job Chapter 2 verse 9, "Then said his wife unto him, Dost thou still retain thine integrity? Curse God, and die."

We can tell she was speaking out of anger. She tried to coach Job on how to die and end to his devotion and purity. It was not in her intention to taking sides with the devil, but she did. She told Job to do what Satan told God that Job would do if He took everything from him. "Satan said to God, but put forth Thine hand now, and touch his bone and his flesh, and he will curse Thee to thy face." Job 2:5

I am so glad the deal was not between God, Satan, and Job's wife. Regardless she told Job to "curse God and die," but it was up to Job to maintain his faith. Wait a minute here, did Satan put these words in Job's wife's mouth? If Satan did, was He trying to use her like He did Eve? The issue was not about Job's wife, just like it was not about Eve. Here, it was about Job and Job alone. However, we need to quote "Job's answer to his wife, But he said unto her, Thou speakest as one of the foolish women speaketh. What? Shall we receive good things at the hand of God, and shall we not receive evil? In all this did not Job sin with his lips." Job 2:10

Amen. Job did not fall into their distractions. He remained focused until the door of blessings opened wide for him. All worked in his favor because he was indeed a true worshipper. He did not let anyone provoke him enough to kill his worship and praise. Lively, yes, he was in his sickness because Job knew that God had him at heart.

CHAPTER SIX

TRUE WORSHIP MELTS GOD'S HEART

The author of the book of Hebrews shared with us in Chapter 12 and verse 6, saying, "For whom the Lord loveth he chasteneth every son whom he receiveth." "And ye have forgotten the exhortation which speaketh unto you as unto children, my son, despise not thou the chastening of the Lord, nor faint when thou art rebuked of Him."

Whatever is going on between you and God is between you and God.

However, I do not want to sound too selfish. I understand perfectly well that your sin and my sin affect more than one person. It involves God and the people who care for us. As far as the people are concerned, their job is to help us pray to God, not judge our sins, and then pray. To pray to God is to worship God. To worship God on someone's behalf is the most significant gift we can ever offer a person.

Why is that? For example, to minister to a sick person is to minister unto God. (Matthew 25:35-40) still, it is up to God to

114

validate or not the ministration. After we prayed, the matter is no longer in our hands, which also goes for persistent prayers. God is continuously operating in his will. When we worship and praise Him that does not give us a free pass to change His Will. However, a contrite mind, body, and soul could indeed melt God's heart, not His Will, because His will shall be done regardless, whether we are choosing to be pioneers of heaven or not.

One of the best stories to me in the Bible that depicts what true worship and praise can do is the story of King Hezekiah in the book of Isaiah Chapter 38. To fully appreciate the power beyond prayer and praise, we must quote the first five verses individually for the sake of commentary. 1) "In those days was Hezekiah sick unto death. And Isaiah the prophet the son of Amos came unto him, and said unto him, Thus saith the Lord, set thine house in order: for thou shall die, and not live."

There are only two types of sickness in the world, according to the word of God. However, one class can easily convert to the other when God seems to neglect or ignore it. In both types of sickness, worshipping God is the key to avoid this conversion. Vital, crucial, and fatal are the nature of those two sicknesses, but God's miracles are known to change their nature. The first phrase of the verse above introduces us to the first sickness, "UNTO DEATH." It reads, "In those days was Hezekiah sick unto death."

We found the second type in the Gospel of John Chapter 11 verse 4 when Jesus said, "When Jesus heard that, he said, this sickness is not unto death, but for the glory of God, that the Son of God might be glorified thereby." The difference between the two sicknesses is that one is unto death and the other is not; however, we need to understand why one is and one is not. Even though both have a common denominator, "MIRACLE." Jesus already explained to us why the sickness was not unto death. It was for glorification purposes. To glorify the Son of God is to worship God. Again, it is all about honoring and praising God. In Hezekiah's situation, his time was up to die as appointed for every man living under the heavens. Only person that can change his status through a temporary amnesty is God. Let us move on with the 2nd verse as a promise. 2) 'Then Hezekiah turned his face toward the wall, and prayed unto the Lord," The man did not argue with the prophet. He believed the word spoken by Isaiah was the Lord's. Hezekiah automatically positioned himself for orderly worship. He knew the power of prayer. How do I know that? It worked for him. To say a prayer to God is one thing. To believe in the God you are praying for without waving is another. Hezekiah was familiar with the time to worship God. Nevertheless, when is the best moment to worship God? Good question? I wonder how many believers know the answer. I heard some say early in the morning, that others believed at six in the evening at noonday, and the most common one is late in the midnight hour. The best time to worship God is at any time, and we would not hurt God's feelings if we chose to say all the time over anytime. The king proved that. Let us eavesdrop in King Hezekiah's prayer in the 3rd verse, 3) "And said, remember now, O Lord, I beseech Thee, how I have walked before Thee in truth and with a perfect heart, and have done that which is good in Thy sight." In humility, he reminded God of his faithfulness toward Him how he devoted himself to God's services. There is nothing wrong with reminding God how faithful we serve Him if we have been faithful. Hezekiah did not ask God for anything. Apparently, before this thunderous prayer, he could have asked God for healing. At this junction, he was expressing his concern about the message from Isaiah about his death. Hezekiah felt that his faithfulness toward God was challenging. To top it all, he also worshiped God with his tears. Remember the sincere tears of a worshipper always affecting God's heart. The Bible said in the 4th verse, "and Hezekiah wept sore." I cannot help myself but believe sincere tears again in the matter of God reveals how the heart feels to others. I am incapable of knowing the nature of anyone else tears, genuine or not; however, God knows. This is my prayer, naively, that everything worshippers of God do before God is real. The 5th verse is about to show us the result of worship in the middle of trouble, and it reads, "Then came the word of the Lord to Isaiah saying, Go and say to Hezekiah thus saith the Lord, the God of David thy father, I have heard thy prayer, I have seen thy tears: behold, I will add unto thy days fifteen years."

That was awesome. Hezekiah's prayer and tears moved God until He, God, recompensed Hezekiah with an additional fifteen years of the longevity of life. Remember, a sincere tearful prayer unto God was and is known to bring favorable results. Psalm 30 verse 2 we saw where David cried unto God, and God healed him. Psalmist, in Psalm 107, verse 13, we learned how the children of Israel cried unto God in their trouble, and God turned around and saved them from their distresses. Worshippers of God hear me, the same formula still works today, but it requires the same thing he then needed, "The purity of heart." If I allowed myself to play with words, I would say, a pure heart is a sincere heart. Let us humble ourselves before God through worship to receive our healing from Him. In sickness, sometimes some of us praise the doctors more than God and place more confidence in the physicians and forget all about God. Some of us invite God into our business after we are on our way to losing, even under defeat. God was and still is a jealous God. Therefore, put Him first in all situations. Look what happened to King Asa in 2nd Chronicles 16, verse 12, "And Asa in the thirty and ninth year of his reign was diseased in his feet, until his disease was exceeding great: yet in his disease he sought not to the Lord, but to the physicians."

Quite a shame, king Asa died much earlier than he should have because he did not turn to God for healing. How many of us acting like King Asa? In the time of sickness, he failed to trust God for healing; instead, we trusted in the physicians. Remember the problems that we are facing, and anything else is never ours, but God's.

Therefore, worshiping the only God can get us out of any given situation if His Will allows it when invited. Unlike with King Hezekiah, who demonstrated how powerful the alliance between worship and praise could be. After he worshipped God, he recovered by God, and he started to praise God, quite a combination. I wrote a praise song one day entitled "My God is able," and it goes like this.

Don't you be discouraged, don't you be dismayed,
When sickness comes into your life
Remember, my God is able.
Oh my God is able, my God is able,
My God is able to carry you through.
Don't you be dismayed,
When tribulation is coming your way.
Let not your heart be trouble,
Remember, my God is able.
Don't you be discouraged,
When sickness is coming into your life.
Please remember, all sickness is not unto death.
Oh, give God the glory, give God the praises.
Give God the Glory. All sickness is not unto death.
Glory Alleluia, Glory Alleluia, Glory Alleluia Amen.

There are instances in the Bible where worship and praising God change the status of the punishment from the wrath to a quick pardon.

On one occasion, God sent the prophet Jonah to the great city of Nineveh to carry a disturbing announcement to the people of that city. The message was so severe and precise until it scared Jonah himself. Jonah charged to preach against the megacity because their wickedness reached God's presence. Jonah did his best to avoid the mission. He chose to take another course of action contrary to God's. But Jonah quickly understood it was either God's way or whale's way. A whale swallowed him. Jonah was worshipping and praising God for his liberation from that whale's belly even in that awkward position. Once again, the combination of worship and praise had softened God's heart on Jonah's behalf. God spoke to that fish, and it vomited the runaway prophet out on dry land. In Chapter 3, we saw that Jonah accepted his assignment to preach to Nineveh a sermon entitled "Yet in forty days, and Nineveh shall be overthrown."

You see, the people of Nineveh did not waste any time. They believed in God. Right then, they called national worship through fasting and wearing sackcloth from the greatest to the least. Do we have any idea how hard it is to get a household to fast and pray at once? These people in Nineveh beat a Spiritual record with their universal worship. When the king of the city heard about it, he took this worship to a higher level. He left his throne, took off his royal robe, instead wore his sackcloth like his people, sat in ashes, and turned the fast into a decree nationwide with the commandment man and beast to wear sackcloth and cry mightily to God. Wow! Quite a story, a demonstration of the power of worship in praise, another word the king said, let everything that has breath call upon the Lord for total repentance. Here again, the worship and praise to God paid off because it reached God's compassionate heart with its sincerity and truthfulness.

Let us put the icing on the cake with verse 10, "And God saw their works, they turned from their evil way; and God repented of the evil, that He had said that He would do unto them; and did it not."

On the other hand, Jonah did not know that the people and the beast made peace with their God. He took a ringside seat where he could be an eyewitness of the destruction of Nineveh. He became unhappy when God changed his mind. Who knows,

Jonah, may feel like God has made a liar out of him before the people? A lying prophet, no Jonah was not when considering God's compassionate heart. What about the scary and disobedient prophet? Jonah, in my opinion, wore the crown.

In today's world, the king would classify as crazy or ignorant some might even accuse him of practicing witchcraft for ordering a beast to be part of the fasting and the crying out unto God. Speaking from experience, I remember on January 12, 2010, when the earthquake- ravaged Port-au-Prince, Haiti, my native land. I was unable to reach my family and my friends, especially my brothers. There was no communication, no electricity, and no food to eat. The earthquake's magnitude forced most to be homeless and destitute in the Capital where my brothers live. I became very disturbed because of a lack of information.

The small amount of news I received caused more harm to my soul than good. Then I turned to different Gospel Stations to hear a word, a prayer from some anointed men and women of God on behalf of the earthquake victims. I was disappointed in my Spirit when I heard men and women of God playing God. They presumed to know the reason why God allowed the earthquake in this Caribbean nation Haiti Thomas.

They concluded that it was because of their sins. If sin were the reason, many other countries would have been in the same boat as Haiti destroyed a long time ago. I know it does not matter how sinful a nation is; there will always be a presence of great men and women of God among her citizens, and because of their presence in that place, God will limit His wrath. Remember in the story of Sodom and Gomorrah, God waited until Lot's Abraham's nephew and his family left Sodom before He destroyed it, Genesis 19:1-11.

When I heard how some Christians judged the country, I led to doing what I knew best for my fellow citizens and brothers. I was ushered into a strange fast where I wore the same clothes repeatedly and went to have prayer at the church three times a day until I heard from my brothers. This was my vow to God, not anyone else's. When I first heard the news about the earthquake, I had on a blue shirt, a pair of blue jeans, and white sneakers. It took me thirty-one days to hear from my brothers. Then I changed my clothes and called off the fast.

I was criticized by some of my peers, who tried to disrupt and distract my worship. Maybe they had forgotten or did not realize that I had met people like them before, which brought me to this dimension in

GOD. Some said I needed to change my clothes because God is a God of cleanliness, and I answered, pray for me. But one thing I knew was that my heart was clean and pure according to God's expectation. When all attempts failed, they associated my way of worship with a witchcraft mentality. I will tell you what God did to answer me through my perseverance. How bad did I want what I needed from the Lord? Badly, and He gave me the desire of my heart just as the citizens and the beasts of the city of Nineveh were well prepared to worship God uniformly in their order of worship. Yes, they were. After this wonderful worship experience, who would not want to devote their time to worshiping God but sometimes being consistent with God is the hardest thing for some worshippers to do, especially when they failed to let maturity and growth take their course in their Spiritual life.

It is a known fact that worshipping God requires patience. Otherwise, worship will be ineffective. The lack of patience is the worshipper's worst enemy because it can potentially kill their anointing. It seemed like the king of Nineveh was anointed overnight. Why would I say that? The type of worship he ordered for his people proved there was some uncultivated anointing dwelling inside him, just as it is in some of us before knowing God. How could that be? I am glad someone asked. The law of agreeing and disagree is now in effect. Remember, when God created man, God blew the breath of life in his nostril, and man became a living soul. Keep in mind that wherever there is a soul, there is a Spirit because God, the owner of all souls, poured out His Spirit in them to give them life. Therefore, everybody is born with a foreordained and unique anointing, which may or may never be activated.

It all is depending on the individual's choice. To develop his anointing, one must understand the uniqueness of worship and its role in sanctification. Moreover, one needs to recognize, accept, and believe God for who He is "The author and finisher of the faith." Again, worship is what activates the anointing. I feel deep in my soul that worship gives birth to the anointing, and the anointing is the heartbeat of praise. The greater the anointing, the higher the praise in a believer's life, but true worship is the main connector for both. It is almost impossible to worship and praise God in the absence of an anointing. Whenever worship and praise are in town, the anointing has no other choice but to show up. Sometimes all it takes is an invitation. Have you ever considered why the Bible emphasizes so much on the manifestation of God's power through miracles? By the hands of those who allow God to activate the pouring of His anointing on them. I am not talking about anointing oil, which serves as an affirmation by God. It is to symbolize the confirmation of the anointed believer. Pure and straightforward, anointing oil is one of the elements of worship regardless of if we believe in it or not. It is what it is, but one thing it is not, it does not make one anointed. It is the emblem of being called.

The king of Nineveh and his people made themselves available to hear from God by reviving and stirring up their anointing through worship. God was well pleased with the changing of their heart, and He spared them from His wrath. That is what I called the power of prayer.

CHAPTER SEVEN

THE EFFECT OF BEING ANOINTED BY GOD

Anointing in the Spiritual meaning can be a touchy subject to discuss with some people. Commonly, when speaking of anointing the first thing that comes to the mind of many is anointing oil, even when looking at the meaning of the word in the dictionary. For this reason, there always will be controversies in the meaning of the word. To some, the practice of anointing oil is vividly important in their lives. On the contrary, others believe this practice in today's world is barbarous and meaningless. It does not matter how one feels about the anointing oil; it does not have anything to do with them being anointed. I practice it in my church, and I also fellowship with others who do not engage in such belief. Some never heard of it, and that does not affect their anointing.

I remember I was at a funeral, but before the service began, I was sitting in the pastor's study with the pastor of the church, and three other pastors waiting for the family to arrive. Suddenly, there was a gentle knock at the door, and the pastor said, come in. The door opened, and it was one of his members. He greeted and introduced her to us. She apologized for her disturbance, and he replied that it was fine. She opened her purse, pulled out a bottle of olive oil, and asked him to pray over it so she could anoint herself for her healing whenever he had the opportunity. He was somewhat disappointed. He took the oil from her, and she left. The pastor was insulted by her request, and he said to us, "Who does she think she is? Did you hear what she asked me to do? I am not going to do it, not unless somebody could show me where, in the New Testament, anointing oil was used on someone that was sick. We are the New Testament Church; Christ died for all that." At this point, he was furious and embarrassed over the situation. Keep in mind, consider my standards, this pastor friend of mine is an anointed Gospel preacher who happens to let his denomination influence his judgment. I told him that evening, I was not trying to change his belief nor persuade him in any way. However, turning the Bible to the Epistle of James chapter 5 verse 14, I read to him concerning the oil. Then he said, "Okay let us pray over the oil." Now I feel more comfortable doing it because I read it for myself." Then, he asked me to say the prayer and I replied, "She asked you, Pastor because she believed in the God that is in you and this faith is what will convert the oil from regular oil to anointed oil. Therefore, do not let her down. Do the prayer, and we will help you?" He did it; afterward, he went and preached the funeral. That evening, God poured out his Spirit on him and the Church as he delivered the word. After the service, he said to me, "That anointing oil did work." "What do you mean, I replied?" He said, I gave her the oil then I asked her could I anoint myself. She said, yes. I stuck my finger in the oil, I anointed my forehead and asked God to give me a fresh anointing. Did you see the result, he asked me? I replied that God would never ignore the prayer of a sincere and righteous' heart. However, it was God's anointing and people displaying the true anointing through obedience. The oil that you prayed for became anointed because it was in the hand of an anointed man of God who believed and asked God to allow it to be so.

One night, I was at a conference given by a religious organization that I was affiliating with. There was a workshop that night and one of the participants asked the lecturer about his opinion on the use of anointing oil in some churches. The lecturer was tickled by the question and sarcastically answered, "Pure madness, and you better not use that mess." Almost everyone in that church was filled with laughter, and I did not know what was so funny. A complete silence invaded the church, and everyone gave him their undivided attention; he said, *let me show you how I feel about oil in the church,* especially on the pulpit. How you call it again, anointing oil, he said comically, then answered his own question. He continued by saying, my son in the ministry invited me to preach his revival at a church where he is the pastor. While I was preaching, I glanced at a bottle of oil good to fry some chicken. In the middle of the sermon, I asked the pastor, what is this you have over there? I pointed to the oil, and he replied, this is anointing oil. I said what, anointing oil. He said yes. I asked him, do you have a garbage can nearby? The pastor replied, right over there. I picked up the oil and threw it into the garbage. I told him nowhere in the New Testament will you find the use of anointing oil on sick believers.

After he was through telling the story, he received a standing ovation from the workshop congregants accompany by some Amen. Then he asked, does anyone have a comment for me? I waved my hand and he made room for me to talk, and I said, with all due respect, I feel that you were arrogant, and you are wrong. I am glad you were not at my church because this behavior would have put an end to our fellowship for throwing something that I considered sacred unto my God into the garbage. Furthermore, you were wrong about the New Testament concerning the anointing oil. If you do not mind, I have scripture in the Epistle of James I would like to share with you guys. Chapter 5 verses 14, "Is any sick among you? Let him call for the elders of the church; and let them pray over him, anointing him with oil in the name of the Lord:" I read it, and I asked him if he could explain what the verse in question meant. He told me, go ahead, and explain it. Politely, I stood up, and by the aid of the Holy Ghost, I was able to show both the congregation and him where he had the right not to believe in anointing oil without being an enemy to those that do.

He was trespassing when he tried to push his belief arrogantly on someone else. Worship is all about respect for the individual worshiper. Because I believe in anointing oil, that does not give me the right to use my anointing oil in a church that I know for a fact does not entertain such practice. Otherwise, I am not showing any respect for the church and their leadership, and I become a self-righteous bully. No one should have used anointing oil in a place that belongs to somebody else without permission from the leader. This is one of the things that I called pulpit and church manners. They are many believers in God who never heard about the practice of anointing oil, because this practice is optional.

The conclusion of this matter is whatever an individual or a church uses to enhance their worship to God is fine by God. Whether it is the use of anointing oil, incense, myrrh, candles, chandelier to beautify the sanctuary, worship music etc., strive to avoid legalism. The rule is simple in the absence of the dictatorship Spirit. Let us respect one other's way of worship to a true living God.

Now let us reason together about being anointed by God. I often heard throughout my Christian journey how people praise the anointing on other people. I heard this statement so many times, "so and so has a beautiful anointing." However, when we ask the question, what is the anointing? We react to the question as if it were a tricky one. The word anointed is a part of our Godly conversation, but the minute someone poses the question to us, some of us automatically enter deep thinking, trying to come up with the answer. Believers swear out that they are anointed but still do not know what the anointing is. The answer is simple, God pouring out His Spirit on the flesh for a particular mission. In other words, it is God's power over the flesh.

Being anointed by God is to be controlled by God. It is a lifestyle. Some call the Spirit, the Holy Spirit. Others call Him the Holy Ghost. I have heard some vain disputation over this name by those who love to argue, just to argue, not knowing they are playing with words. Whether some choose to call Him the Holy Ghost, others the Holy Spirit, at the end of the day, they are talking about the Spirit of God. This type of argument is what I called denomination distraction based on a divisional confusion. Anyway, to be beneficiaries of the pouring out of the Spirit of God required confession from the mouth and believing from the heart with all sincerity that Jesus is the only begotten Son of God. He died for your sins and to accept Him as your Lord and savior.

Trust me, if you are heavenly bound and the anointing which was dormant in you because of sinful disobedience is automatically reactivated by God. Do not let anyone rob you from who you are in God and from what God is to you in your life.

The minute you have been fulfilled, all the formalities require to be restored and reinstalled into God's family by God Himself. You have become ordained and anointed which means, set apart for the services of God. This good news is enough to make anyone that knows about God's goodness to shout with joy, "Thank God for Jesus." When I made mention of being set apart, I am not talking about preaching the gospel only, but, if need be, so be it. For too long, the tradition made some of us believe being ordained and being anointed is something reserve for preachers and deacons only. It is not so. Remember, these two offices are supposed to be the least in the house of God. Most people might consider the sexton's occupation as the least in the church while it is the greatest. An anointed sexton is a force to be working with. I learned a long time ago, the higher you are in the house of God, the more of a servant you must be to the people. Again, whatever we do for the Lord must be done with the anointing because we are ordained to do it that way.

On a biblical level, let us shed more light about being anointed by God. In the book of Joel, we see where God said, "I will pour out My Spirit upon all flesh;" Joel 2:28. This statement alone proves that the word discrimination is not in God's vocabulary. It proves again that God has enough Spirit to pour out on everyone who is willing to receive Him. The same Spirit turns into an anointing in the life of those who accept Him.

Being anointed by God is a unique affair. No two anointing are alike even though they come from the same Spirit. However, being anointed attracts malicious criticism, diversity, adversity, jealousy, and controversy and covetousness. The reason for that we often concentrate on someone else's anointing instead of our own. Apostle Peter offers great advice. He says, "Wherefore laying aside all malice, and all guile, and hypocrisies and envies, and all evil speaking, As new born babes, desire the sincere milk of the word, that ye may grow thereby: If so be ye have tasted that the Lord is gracious." I Peter 2: 1-3

Being anointed is a growing process, but the growth is up to the recipient. All depend on the company he keeps and his availability to let God use him for the service of God.

Now let us view somewhat in detail the effect of the anointing upon a believer and its seal of approval by God. Before going any further, a few questions demand answers. Those questions are great but argumentative and distractive, surrounded by legalism. The answers to those questions could be passionate and touchy. Touchy to the point of causing someone to discontinue the reading of this manuscript, even to set it on fire. Allow me to say a word of prayer before dealing with those issues, "Father God have mercy, in Jesus' name I pray Amen,"

Does someone have to speak in tongue to be anointed by God? The answer is "NO" with a capital letter.

Is speaking in other tongues an element of being called? "YES" in all the meaning of the word because being anointed is evidence of worship.

Does speaking in tongue have anything to do with the redeeming quality? The answer again is "NO."

Is speaking in other tongues rude when speaking in public without an interpreter? The answer is "NO."

Here comes the verdict, either way, I am in hot water because not too many believers could digest the truth. The conclusion of this matter is, if God blessed a believer with a Spiritual language, please use it to edify God. Avoid pointing fingers at those who are ignorant of the language. On the other hand, if someone does not believe in such language, please do not criticize, or associate him with modern day barbarous.

I was at a worship service in a church that did not believe in the practice of speaking in tongue. The presence of God was in the service. Suddenly, a young lady who was a member of that church overrode all the rules of sophistication that they adhered to. She was in the Spirit. She began to speak in an unknown tongue. It was the first time she ever experienced speaking such an awesome language. Keep in mind; she was not stepping out of the water after being baptized. That night, by the grace of God, when she spoke in tongue, I understood everything she said. The Pastor of the church and some of his congregants were agitated by her behavior. If cutting the eyes at somebody could kill, she would have died. He whispered under his breath, "This will be the last time she brings that mess into my church; we are not..." and he mentioned the name of a church denomination in his statement. Another competitive mind in action, "My Faith is better than yours." The Spirit of religious competition is also known as witchcraft because it causes so-called believers to be manipulatives. They feel the need to bring someone under the subjection to their ways of worship. This is manipulation, and manipulation equals witchcraft. I whispered in his ears; God sent a message to you by the young lady. He looked at me as if to say; I am about to get you off my pulpit with your roots working self. I continued, "Do not look at me like this," and he said, incredulously, she is on the floor, bringing embarrassment to herself. "How am I supposed to get the message? I cannot understand a word she is saying?" "God gave me the interpretation; I replied," "she said through the Spirit of God that you had been diagnosed with cancer, and you hid it from your wife, your children, your church family, and your friends. Monday, when you go to the doctor, you will be cancer-free." "I did not give him a chance to answer me back. The service was reaching its end. I got up, shook everybody's hand, and congratulated the Evangelist for the night for a well-prepared message from the Lord. I looked back at the pastor, and I told him to give me a call on Monday after his visit." The Pastor glared at me in amazement as though he has seen a ghost. Oh well, this is one of the effects of being anointed. I left the church and later it was told to me that he thanked the lady for allowing God to use her. He, then, gave his testimony and apologized to his wife. I felt blessed, the Pastor did not tell the people who translated the message for him. On that Monday, he found out from his doctor that he was cancer-free.

I am telling the story to say that the gifts that we receive from God are never designed to make one feel superior to another inferior. (Big I and little u.) All the gifts, including speaking in tongues, come under one umbrella, Spiritual gifts, and they operate differently on each worshipper. Let me make another point of awareness. I speak a few languages. I have learned that any language spoken can indeed be interpreted. This rule also goes for the speaking in the tongues. However, it is unfortunate that some folks are only interested in speaking in tongues to prove they have the Holy Ghost or the Holy Spirit. They forget to petition God for the ability to interpret this fantastic language. Some of us deprive, limit, and alienate ourselves from asking for it based on limitation status. Speaking in tongue, it is only suitable for edification and a tool to attack an adversary. We dwell on inconsequential things; for example, who baptizes in the name of the Father, the Son, and the Holy Spirit or in the name of Jesus Christ instead?

The devil is a liar, and he tries to promote rivalries in the body of Christ. Did I say the devil tries? I better rephrase my statement; he does a good job distracting and dividing us with words or phrases with the same meaning but is written in other forms. Apostle Paul for example never condemned the speaking in the tongue in public. He only offered other avenues of awareness that speaking in the tongue can be interpreted. I am a witness to that fact. Gifts from God require obedience, humility, fasting, and praying; in word "WORSHIP." It is all about relationships. Another example is when people say the Holy Ghost versus the Holy Spirit, is it the truth that I am talking about two different Persons? One group indicates that we save if we receive the Holy Spirit, and another group thinks it means we are on our way to hell if we say Holy Spirit rather than Holy Ghost! Madness, yes, this is religious madness to even think of such a distinction. One day, I stumbled on a conversation between two individuals where someone proclaimed that a particular religion is going to hell because they believe in the Holy Spirit instead of the Holy Ghost. God forgive me, but I laughed so hard because I thought I was in a comedy show where people talked nonsense. Two weeks later, I overheard a member of the group that believed in the Holy Spirit argued with another person and said, "if you believe in the Holy Ghost, you might as well kiss heaven goodbye because in hell you will lift your eyes."

Lord have mercy. I thought our job is to fight the devil as a team. Instead, we are fighting against one another over vain belief caused by man's wisdom and have nothing to do with salvation. This type of argument is not in my book line up with the word of God. Spiritual ego is nothing other than the devil's servants. There is nothing wrong with having faith in God and in having religious preference.

The danger is when we embrace the idea that anyone having faith in God who is not a part of our denomination will go to hell. As long as God is the center that is what really counts. Let us not allow a few scriptures taken out of context to divide us forever. At a time, we are guilty of misusing, misquoting, misunderstanding, and misinterpreting the scriptures of the Bible. Just hold fast to the faith that we choose without judging others' faith, especially when we all believe in the one true God. Indeed, if we worship Him with a pure heart, he will lead us and guide us into truth. In cases where people do not believe in God, let us introduce them to God if they allow us to without confusing them the more with our division over scriptures as if we serve a divided God. There is nothing wrong with thinking that we are the only sheep in God's fold, but the minute He tells us that we are not the only one and one day He will bring the other sheep unto the fold. Then, we need to understand that we might have different creed as far as scriptures are concerned whenever we meet. However, we will have one thing in common we all will know without a shadow of a doubt that Jesus is our Shepherd. John 10:16

To fully understand the anointing of God that overshadows us, we must understand the faith process to avoid blasphemy against the Holy Ghost or Spirit does not be quick to judge. I am about to give an illustration which might be profitable. If the question was asked, how do we like our eggs cooked? Personally, I would say scrambled or boiled, some might say boiled, others might say raw, while others prefer fried hard or overlay. To me, some of the choices are nasty. Still, I need to respect the people who love their eggs raw or overlay. I can eat my eggs the way I like them without criticizing how others eat them. In the end, we are all eating eggs. So, it is with the Spirit of God. We worship through the same Spirit, and because we do things differently in worship, and they are beyond our understanding. It does not mean what we are doing does not line up with God's word. Unless we have prayed in Satan's name then we know for a fact we are not lining up with the word of God. Then we know for a fact that we are not talking about Christianity.

When God anoints us, we are anointed indeed. He called us to do great things in his name after being ordained. God does not anoint us to go somewhere and sit down in the seat and do nothing. When Jesus called the first disciples, He called them to be missionaries because He had a mission for them. Remember Jesus ordained the twelve disciples to be with Him so He could send them to preach and to have the power to heal the sick and cast out devils, Mark 3:14, 15. When God clothes us with His anointed through His Spirit, everything in us and out of us becomes powerful sometimes until death, especially the words from the hearts, which proceed out of our mouths. Worshipping God daily in all sincerity with the practice of fasting and praying could trigger this type of anointing from God into our lives. Again, we cannot let anyone rob us of this way of life because the effect of being anointed is the demonstration of God's power into our beings. Again, the effect of the anointing is a believer exercising their faith in God through worship and praise. Another effect of the anointing is Jesus

Christ who left us a Comforter who is the Holy Ghost or the Holy Spirit to abide permanently in us, and with us until the day of the Lord. His mission is to lead us, guide us, and keep us, and with that belief no one could ever distract us from worshipping God unless we allow it. From the Old Testament to the New Testament, let study the manifestation and the power of the anointing.

CHAPTER EIGHT

THE MANIFESTATION AND THE POWER OF THE ANOINTING

The Anointer and the Giver of the anointing, who is God, make sure that those faithful and obedient to Him possess an everlasting anointing even their remains after the physical death. Many might disagree with me because of the teaching that after death, there is no sound left in the flesh, it decayed, and the bones dry up. Let us see if, through the scripture, we can reach an agreement on the subject. I am a firm believer that our anointing never dies but that it goes into stages of remission because of self-praise and disobedience to God. Sometimes we can be too wrapped up in our anointing that we forget all about the Anointer and consume by the gift that we completely ignore the Giver, who is God. Being anointed is a blessing, and we should never forget to worship and praise God from whom all gifts filter in and out. Also, I am a firm believer that whatever God does for one of his anointed, He could also do it for another according to their calling. Let me clarify something about the anointing. The anointing of God on believers does not manifest Himself equally on His recipients. For example, some may be anointed to preach, to sing, to prophecy, to minister, to teach, to work miracles, to interpret dreams, visions, and tongues, and the list goes on and on until it is impossible for a believer's anointing not to be on the list. Some may have more of the anointing than others, but they all fall under one umbrella and are all equally important to God, and all are the products of true worship through the power of the anointing. This is God's theocracy.

There was a mighty Prophet in the Old Testament by the name of Elisha. He was very much anointed. The Bible said that Elisha died and he was buried and something impressive happened so impressive that I must quote it, "And it came to pass, as they were burying a man, that, behold, they spied a band of men; and they cast the man into the sepulcher of Elisha: and when the man was let down, and touched the bones of Elisha, he revived, and stood up on his feet," 2 Kings 13: 21.

You see what I mean, the man and the woman of God who is in good standing with God anointed until and after death. God's anointing on a true worshipper affects everything around the worshipper, his clothes, his language, walk, demeanor and his devotion. In other words, everything around that worshipper is subject to benefit from the worshipper's anointing. For example, let us look at a similar case. In the New Testament, there was a woman with an issue of blood. She had been sick twelve long miserable years, seeking healing. She tried everything, and nothing worked. All the doctors she visited were unable to cure her but, there was one thing she had not attempted in her endeavor, and that was "Worship." The Bible said that when she had heard that Jesus was passing through, she took conscience of her situation and condition behind Jesus; she found herself among some overprotective disciples and a curious crowd. She did not want to be in that position, but her frail body denied her access to be in the presence of Jesus. She was too weak to penetrate the uncompassionate crowd. She made a statement of faith in herself that deserved to be quoted, "For she said, if I may touch but His clothes, I shall be whole."

Quite a belief! When she did touch Jesus, immediately, she knew she had the victory over her plague. Suddenly, He felt her touch and His anointing healed her. Worship is personal, and God is the only one who understands it. The disciples did not see the woman touching Jesus because it was not their business, even though they tried to make it their affairs when Jesus said, "Who touched my clothes?" If we are familiar with the story, we will observe how they tried to distract Jesus by putting their two cents in this woman and her Lord's affair. Jesus knew what came out of Him and when He looked around and saw the woman. She came, and fell before Him, and told Him the truth. She demonstrated her faith, and she was elevated from a certain woman as the Bible began the story to a daughter after she met Jesus. A beautiful story Mark 5:25-34 "if you have not already, I suggest you read it." Despite of everything, her position behind Jesus was not that bad because she ended up in front of Him through His compassion. By the way, this is the ninth recorded miracle of Jesus.

Now we see two similar stories from two different Testaments that brought about the same result. The point I am making here, is that some of the miracles that we see occur in the Old Testament occurred in the New Testament and continue to happen in today's world amongst the worshippers of God. As long as worshippers continue to worship God in Spirit and truth, miracles, signs, and wonders will continue to manifest through gifts that God bestows upon those who worship him. Again, worship attracts miracles, signs, and wonders. Can we find worship in the miracles performed by our Savior? Let us find out.

In the first recorded miracle of Jesus, He turned water into wine at a wedding. Notice in the story that when his mother told Him there was no wine, his answer to Mary was "his hour was not yet come." Still his mother advised the servants to do whatever He asked them to do. John 2:1-10

Agree or disagree, I have a great deal of respect for his mother, who introduced those servants to two of the essential rules of worship, which are our faith and obedience. No one can ever go wrong when doing what God tells them to do and have faith to believe it is a done deal. The biggest problem facing worshippers is the idea of doing what the Spirit commanded them to do, especially if it is something that required them to step out on faith. His mother and the servant exercised their faith and obedience in Jesus. The elements of this miracle required water.

In the Old Testament, Moses and Aaron obeyed the voice of God. They did smite the waters from the river and the waters turned into blood. That was what God told them to do with the rod in the presence of Pharaoh and his servants, Exodus 7:20. The same God that turned water into blood also turned it into wine.

People of God, if we eliminate the Old Testament, and only embrace the New Testament we violate of God's theocracy.

The Bible is the greatest and the most extensive library in the world. It divides into two distinct parts the Old and the New Testament. The Old Testament begins with the book of Genesis, ends with the book of Malachi, while the New Testament begins with the book of Matthew and ends up with the book of Revelation. I say all this to make this point If anybody has a problem with Genesis 1:1 through Malachi 4:5, they certainly have a problem with Matthew 1:1 through Revelation 22:21.

We learned that when the sun was going down; in the second miracle was that our Savior went on a healing spree. With one particular medicine, He healed all manner of sickness. What was the medicine that he used? His bare hands, He laid them on everyone and healed them, Luke 4:40

Jesus again teaches that our anointing has no border, no limitation when God chooses us for exceptional work or works. In all the body parts, the hands seemed to have the upper hand in Spiritual power. When it touches someone or something unclean, it is converted to cleanliness by the power of God. So far, we have learned that miracles are performed by connecting using the hands. Let us not be afraid to use our hands on the sick if we feel and know it is a major part of our anointing through worship.

The third miracle demonstrates the power of worship and how it attracts compassion from our Savior. In Matthew 8:1-4, we learned that when Jesus came down from the mountain and a multitude was following Him and suddenly, came a leper, and the leper worshiped Jesus by demonstrating his faith. He said "Lord, if thou wilt, canst thou make me clean." Jesus touched him, saying I will; be thou clean. The Bible said that, immediately, his leprosy was cleansed. Look what Jesus said; He charged the man not to tell anyone. However, Jesus wanted him to go and show himself to the priest and offer the gift commanded by Moses for a testimony unto them. Here the Bible does not give a reason behind this man's leprosy. However, in the Old Testament, we find where Aaron and Miriam questioned Moses's leadership. As we know, this behavior is well known in the Spiritual realm. The disunion among them was so terrible until God had to intervene. God was upset with them. Miriam Moses' sister became leprous because of her criticism against God's servant Moses. Aaron quickly asked Moses to forgive them for their foolishness. In Aaron's mind, he thought Moses was the one who had done it. He petitioned Moses to spare her life. Look how meek Moses was; instead of him holding a grudge, he cried unto God on her behalf and begged God to heal her, and God cured her of leprosy. Her foolishness distracted and delayed their journey for seven days, Numbers 12:9-16.

This is another miracle through worship. We could learn a great lesson from that story and stop creating confusion around each other where God has to intervene. For this reason alone, many are sick today for criticizing and bad-mouthing the servants of God. Both miracles were about leprosy, and both healed miraculously. In the first example, our Savior showed great respect for the Mosaic Law. Now we can agree that Jesus never teaches anyone to overlook nor disobey the Old Testament. One of His missions was to fulfill the law not to abolish it. The Old Testament miracles were never based on the law of the Old Testament. So why do some of us want to classify everything under the law? In this miracle, Jesus made sure the man offered the gift commanded by Moses. Here is a profitable recommendation, I would suggest that every believer adopt the idea that after healing by God, knowing that he healed us and freed us from doctor bills, we would bring a monetary gift in the name of Jesus to the church of our affiliation. If we are not members of any church, give it to a charity or organization where it could use for the glory of God. I know from experience that healing offerings work, and it is far cheaper than hospital and doctor's bills. Bless God for everything He does for us.

The man worshiped Jesus by faith, and Jesus reminds him to observe one of the elements of worship which, is giving.

In Miriam's leprosy dilemma, we see how Moses interceded to God on her behalf, and she was healed from her leprosy. Now let us see how a Centurion will intercede on behalf of a servant that is dear to him.

The 4th Miracle through worship of Jesus happened when a centurion had a servant that was dear to him that was sick unto death. When he heard about Jesus, he begged the elders to ask Jesus if he would heal his servant. When they met Jesus, the elders tried to give Jesus a reason why He should do this for the Centurion; he built them a synagogue. The elders of the Jews underestimated the faith of the Centurion, not knowing that he had more faith in Jesus than all of them. Sometimes that is the way it is in the church. We expect the Church Officers to have more faith than all of us because of who they are. I am here to say, the position you occupy in the church has nothing to do with faith because faith comes by believing in God and His Word, and from that belief is born an unweaving relationship with God through worship. The Centurion sent friends to tell Jesus does not bother to come to his house because he was not worthy to receive such a great personality as Jesus. The Centurion, in a way, explained why he did not come to Jesus himself instead of sending a messenger. He felt he was unworthy to be in the presence of Jesus. I sympathize with the centurion because I know that feeling, but I thank God for worship and praise. The Centurion said to Jesus "but say in a word, and my servant shall be healed." When Jesus heard these things, the Bible tells us that Jesus marveled at the Centurion's faith. "Jesus said He had not found so great faith in Israel," Luke 7:2-9.

Does our faith through worship marvel Christ or humanity? Let us make sure our faith marvels at Christ by believing in Him.

The 5th miracle of Jesus depicts how He healed Simon's mother-in-law of a fever when coming from the synagogue with Simon, Andrew, James, and John. When they went into the house, they saw her sick. They did not waste any time calling on Jesus, and this was the right attitude.

Some of us missed out on our healing for failing to call on Jesus first instead of 911 or a next-door neighbor or family member to rush us to the hospital. Learn to call on Jesus first, and He will direct our path on what to do next. Remember, it only takes a few seconds to call on Jesus when the going gets tough. I remember going to see a friend who had surgery. She was at her house. When I got there, she was in severe pain. She asked me to pray for her healing and I did. In the meantime, her five-year-old daughter came in the room, gave hugged me, and with a serious look, she glanced at her mother, and she said, "Mommy, are you in pain?" her mother answered, "Yes, baby, I am, but I still want a kiss from you." She went and kissed her mother. That little girl blew my mind while kissing her mother; she asked, "Can I pray to Jesus for you, you know he can take the pain away and you will feel much better." To me it was the most beautiful thing I had ever heard from a child. She was so serious about her belief because of her upbringing. Her mother said, "Yes, baby, even though the Pastor prayed already, I could get another prayer from my princess." She looked at me and said,

"Would you help me pray, Pastor Pierre? I said sure, and my heart was excited to hear the prayer from the heart of a five-year-old. She started the prayer by saying, "Jesus, I know you have already healed my mommy, but I am asking you to remove the pain from her" on this, she ended the prayer. Her prayer, especially the sincerity of it moved my heart. I asked her, "Who taught you to worship God the way you do." She pointed at her father and mother. She said, "they told me to call on Jesus whenever I need something special, they said you say Jesus always gives good gifts to people that love Him." That evening, I came to the unlimited conclusion; there is no healing without pain and suffering. Anything that causes grief to a believer who trusts God is nothing but the steps to true happiness.

The disciples shared the news with Jesus; immediately, He came into the house, took Peter's mother-in-law by the hand, lifted her, and the fever left her. A touch from Jesus healed her, and to show her gratitude toward God, she got up and ministered unto them. Mark1:29-31

She had to do what she had to do because she knew who healed her body and she showed her appreciation by ministering unto them. Why couldn't these disciples have prayed for her themselves? We need to understand they were still in training and were learning to heal in the name of the master Teacher Himself. They had not yet reached the maturity to fully believe in Christ. When we have a strong belief in God, we spontaneously call on Him when facing a problem and He often comes to our rescue.

There is one thing that I have trouble understanding, and I often wondered why sometimes the people who do not have that much knowledge in the word of God often have more faith in God than those of us who educate in the word. It appears it should be the other way around. I Remembered years ago; I went back to my native land Haiti to visit family and longtime friends. While I was there, my father took sick while he was preparing himself to take his shower. When I looked at him, I saw him slowly going down on his knees, and he fell to the ground. My baby brother was also visiting at the time. We both saw what happened, we ran toward our father, and we said to him in unison, father, are you ok? are you ok? We did not get an answer. My oldest brother, who lived there with him, came running between us and grabbed him, saying, "Lord Jesus, I need you now." At his saying my father opens his eyes saying, "thank you, Lord." I was so happy for my father, so proud of my oldest brother, so ashamed, and so embarrassed of myself. I felt guilty for not calling on Jesus first as my brother did. Because I am one of his ministers who often taught others to call on Him first in times of need. The happiness that I had over my brother's reaction, overshadow my guilt. I was able to apologize to my God for failing the test. My father was healed instantly that day. Then I said to my oldest brother that was some faith you exemplified here today, calling on Jesus first. He answered me, saying, "To God be the glory, it is not what you teach us to do to think of Jesus first in any given situation, and He will answer you one way or another." My oldest brother helped me reach the place in God that I enjoy today; when it came to lips services, I was your man, but I had a long way to go when it came to putting words into action. Since that day, I understand and practice this life-saving statement use God first in all situations. If some of us have not tried it yet, please do because it works. Never underestimate a believer of God as far as miracles are concerned because it is a seasonal gift that works for believers. It all depends on how long their season lasts; only God knows.

The 6th miracle teaches us not to be helpless. I believe the disciples would have made Jesus' day if they had attempted to rebuke the winds themselves. They recognized the power of Jesus, but they deprived themselves of the power they had in Christ. They did not know their worth even with the Savior dwelling amongst them. This is the problem average worshippers have in today's Church, and they are not fully aware of the power they possess when in the presence of God. Even when they are in the presence of God, they still wish to be in God's presence. It sounds dreadful when they say, "In God's presence is where they want to be." They always need to believe no matter where they are, and they are still in the presence of God because He promises to be with them always. Could we imagine worshipping God in the absence of God? If God were not present, it means the worshipper worshipped some other god that is incapable of being omnipotent, omnipresent, and omniscient. The accurate way to get God's attention is through worship and praise.

The disciples were on the ship with Jesus, and they were facing a dangerous tempest. The waves covered the boat. Jesus was sleeping at the time. Instead of the disciples praying for the storm to cease, they went and worshipped Jesus asking Him to save them less they die. Jesus questioned their fear and their faith then, He rose and rebuked both the wind and the sea, and a great calm invaded the ship, Matthew 8:23-26.

God does give us a measure of faith, but it is up to us to develop it to a greater magnitude. Being fearful is the anguish of faith. Being frightened is a choice we make because this is one of the Spirits God never gives to any of His believers. However, God is the only Being we ought to fear, and when that happens, knowledge and wisdom will follow us.

In The Old Testament, we saw where the sea also obeyed God. God caused the sea to go back using a strong east wind, turning the sea into a highway by dividing it. This all took place because of Moses' obedience to God. He stretched out his hand over the sea Exodus 14:21.

God could have done that alone, but he wanted to show Moses the great things he could do by Him, and that goes for all of us. So far, all these miracles have demonstrated relationships between God and His believers. In addition, these miracles are still taking place today in a Spiritual form amongst worshippers. Our biggest problem is that we believe too much in the unbelievers who knock miracles and faith healing down. I learned a long time ago never to believe an unbeliever.

The 7th Miracle speaks for itself, and it proves even the devil knows the power of worship. This why he always tries to rob worshippers of their worship because he is sure worship can and will defeat him. Therefore, he uses one of his best techniques is distraction, to distract worshippers who have yet to reach maturity in remaining focus.

In this Miracle, Jesus met a man with an unclean Spirit, and these types of Spirits are still in existence today. However, not too many believers can deal with them or cast out because of a lack of relationship with God.

The unclean Spirit saw Jesus coming afar off, he ran and worshiped Him. He had more faith in God sarcastically speaking than some of us and knew how to worship and praise God in such a practical way until I must quote him saying to Jesus's word for word in Mark chapter 5:7 "And cried with a loud voice, and said, What have I to do with Thee, Jesus, Thou Son of the Most High God? I ajure Thee by God, that Thou torment me not."

Jesus commanded that unclean Spirit to come out of the man, and he asked him for his name. He told Jesus his name was Legion because they were many. He asked Jesus not to expel him from the country and our Savior granted him his request in Mark 5: 1-19.

Here comes an important point, if God answered an unclean Spirit and satisfied his request, what about us who worship Him constantly. The power is in our hands, but some of us are afraid to use it and let others make us feel powerless. Throughout the Bible God is taking His time to teach and train us how to control the devil and exercise the authority He gives us over anything contrary to His Will and Word.

In the 8th Miracle, a palsied man with incredible faith healed. That Miracle indicates to us; it does not matter how we get to Jesus as long we get there. They were trying to bring a man who was sick with palsy to Jesus to heal. The men that came to get him were confronted with an obstacle in the house. The multitude blocked the entrance door, so they decided to bring the man from the top of the house and let him through with his bed before Jesus. When Jesus saw their faith, He forgave the man's sins and ordered him to pick his bed and go home. Luke 5: 19 - 26.

Was that amazing after the sick man met with Jesus, he did not need anybody to help carry him nor his bed. He carried his own bed. He came to Jesus in one form and left in another through the worshipping power of miracle.

The envious Spirits of the scribes and the Pharisees are still fellowshipping and manifested among us today. They do not believe in signs and wonders done by the hands of men and women of God through their relationship with God without associating it with witchcraft and unbelief. God bless the believers who do not allow these types of mentalities to affect their abilities to perform miracles, signs, and wonders through the worship of God.

In the 9th miracle is the woman with the issue blood that we covered earlier.
The ten miracle was the raising of Jairus' daughter from the dead. This is another miracle, which proves again the excellent relationship existing between worship and miracle.

Jairus was a ruler in the synagogue. He fell on his knees at Jesus's feet and begged Him to come to his house because his only child, his twelve years old daughter, was on the verge of dying. A few seconds later, someone from his home brought him the news that his daughter was dead and that he should not trouble the Master. Jesus told

Jairus not to worry but just believe, and she would be healed. When He arrived at the home He took with Him Peter, James, John, and the father. Jesus said to them that wept that the girl was not dead she was sleeping. They made fun and laughed at Him, and He put them out and raised her from the dead Luke 8:41 - 56.

Jesus had no other choice but to put them out of the house before they became a hindrance to the miracle.

In the Old Testament, Elisha raised a child also from the dead in 2 King chapter 4, and this kind of miracle is happening today by the same Spirit of God.

The 11th miracle depicts worship again. By now, the point that I'm trying to make should have been well digested. It is about two blind men who followed Jesus asked Him to have mercy on them. When Jesus arrived at the house their persistence allowed them to follow Jesus there. Jesus asked them if they believed that He could do this. They answered yes, Lord and Jesus healed them according to their faith Matthew 9: 27- 30.

Whatever we need from the God that we serve is in our faith and our beliefs in Him. Worship is the easiest and the shortest route to get there because worship, strengthens our relationship with God.

In the Old Testament we saw where the man of God used his power in God to cause blindness on an army.

The 12th Miracle showed the ignorance and immaturity of some believers. How deep could we be in our ignorance when we believe in one part of the Bible, and choose to refute the other part? The saddest moment in a so-called believer's life was when they witnessed one of God's miracles. Instead of glorifying God, they chose to credit it to the devil. This mentality is one of the worst cases of blasphemy against the Holy Ghost or the Holy Spirit. It does not matter which Name we choose to call the third Person of the Trinity. One fact remains, a blasphemy to take the work of God and accredited to the devil. There is a warning out for such sin; check it out in Exodus 20: 7 & Matthew 12:31, 32.

Again, why are we so quick to criticize those making themselves available to God to be used mightily by God? The minute God works a miracle by the hands of the open vessel, he or she became an outcast in our sight, which labeled them as worshippers of the devil. Knowledge in God is power, but ignorance of God is vicious, jealous, and contagious. Look what took place in this miracle; they brought to Jesus a man who was dumb, and demon possessed. Jesus cast out the demon, and the man received his speech. The people were amazed, saying this was the first time they ever saw something like this in Israel. A miracle of such magnitude should have made everyone glorify and praise God. However, they were a few unhappy spectators hiding behind the believers. They were the Pharisees. They accused Jesus of casting out devils through the prince of the devils Matthew 9: 32-34. Let me rephrase that they were believers but not true believers because there is a difference between them.

The 13th Miracle deals with a man with a withered hand. Jesus went into their synagogue, and the man with the withered hand was there. Maybe he was there for healing, but one thing we know for a fact is that the Pharisees were using him to entrap Jesus. They were planning a malicious entrapment for Jesus. They asked Him, is it lawful to heal on the Sabbath days? As the story went on, Jesus commanded the man to stretch out his hand, he did, and his hand restored to normal Matthew 12: 9-13

As far as Jesus was concerned, the answer was yes, because He went ahead and did what He had to do. What better time to work miracles other than on the Lord's Day. Whenever there is a worship service, miracles are subject to happen in the life of those who have faith in God.

A similar Miracle took place in the Old Testament in the life of king Jeroboam when his hand was withered, after calling himself retaliating against the man of God in the house of God. The man of God had to entreat God for Jeroboam as he requested of him. The man of God did pray on his behalf, and God restored Jeroboam's hand to normal in 1 King 13:1- 6. This Miracle sends a warning out to us to be careful how we treat men and women of God who are in good relationships with God. I am not referring to the ecclesiastical world whenever I mentioned men and women of God. I am speaking of true believers of God.

The 14th Miracle still supports the power of worship when the disciple took the lunch of an unselfish little boy who had two fish and five loaves of bread and gave them to Jesus who looked toward heaven, gave thanks to God, and as a result, Jesus fed five thousand people. The fish and the loaves kept on multiplying that day, John 6: 1 - 13.

A similar miracle again through worship took place in the Old Testament when a man from Baalshalisha brought his tithing of bread, twenty loaves, and full ears of corn to the man of God. Elisha asked his servant to feed the people, and the servant was reluctant to do so because it was not enough to serve everyone. The man of God insisted that the servant to serve the people because God told the man of God they would have enough and some leftover, and the loaves were multiplying that day according to God's words 2 Kings 4: 42 - 44.

The miracle of God will never fade away as long as we worship Him in Spirit and in truth through faith to believe there is no such thing as impossible in God.

The 15th Miracle teaches us that faith in God is unstoppable, and it is unlimited, but it requires faithfulness to God on our part. To pray is to worship. In the word, we see where Jesus was in prayer; apparently, the ship was still docking, but by the time He ended His worship, the ship capped sail left Him behind. He saw the boat, and it was far away. They were toiling in rowing because the wind was not in cooperation with them.

Awareness speaking, I wondered why the wind started to act up if that was because they left Jesus behind like some of us often do.

The Bible said Jesus came to them walking on the water. They were misidentified by Jesus and His capabilities like we often are when He manifests Himself.

The disciples thought He was a ghost until He advised them to be happy and not to be afraid. Soon Jesus got on board the wind ceased, and they were amazed beyond measure, Mark 6: 46 - 52.

In 2 Kings 6:5, 6, we learned about an ax head that fell in the water, and God worked a miracle by the hand of Elisha, allowing the iron to swim.

The 16th Miracle addressed clearly that true worship does melt God's Heart by triggering and displaying His compassion. A woman of Canaan came to Jesus and called Him by His full name. She came to seek healing for her daughter. Jesus did not answer her. Again, the disciples came and tried to take the matter to a higher-level demanding Jesus to send her away because her worship was too loud. This behavior and Spirit coming from the disciples should not surprise us because it manifests itself among church leaders today through jealousy over worship. She addressed Jesus as she knew Him for herself.

Jesus explained to both the woman and the disciples of His missions, but she came and worshipped Jesus, saying, "Help me." She used two of the most powerful words in worship when worshipping God, "Help me." I cannot keep up with how many times I used the exact two words in addressing my God.

Jesus let her know it was not fair for Him to cast the children's bread to the dogs, and perfectly she agreed with Jesus, but she took her plaint to another notch by saying the dogs eat of the crumbs which fall from their masters' table. Wow! Quite a distinguish faith came out of a sinner's heart and proceeding from her lips, this is indeed what I call the power of worship and praise.

Jesus said to her, "O woman, great is thy faith: Be it unto thee even as thou wilt." Instantly the girl was healed," Matthew 15: 22 - 28.

She used her worship to get what she wanted, and this attitude should not go unnoticed. Therefore, whatsoever we need from the Lord is in our worship, beware of the worship killers who do not mind stopping us from getting closer to God with their vain and envious belief.

CHAPTER NINE

WORSHIP A CONSTANT REMINDER

Worship is a constant reminder to those who do not soon forget. It often reminds us how gracious and compassionate our God is toward us. It also reminds us how impressive and vital God's Fatherhood skills are in our lives. In our daily living, He exercises His duty as a father through His provisional care toward us, His children. Because of the hardening of our hearts, some of us, seem to forget too easily the promises made by God to us in times when we need them the most. The miracles that He does before our eyes are written for our learning seem to be forgotten like yesterday newspaper. We need to keep in mind what God did yesterday, He is well capable of doing it again today, tomorrow, and centuries to come. Why is that? The answer is simple and exciting because God is God.

Strange as it may sound, the people who frequently forget about the capabilities of God are those who are around Him and His words. They have faith issues that paralyzed their belief to the point of death.

Let us glance at the 17th Miracle for a minute. My purpose in this subject is to demonstrate that worship is what activates and generates miracles from God. This miracle is a repeat. This time, the only difference involved four thousand people who had been with Jesus for three days straight fasting and they were hungry. Jesus, the provider that He is refused to send the people home on an empty stomach because they came from far away. The disciples reminded Jesus in a way that they were in the wilderness, and there was not any way a man could satisfy these men with bread.

I believe the disciples had forgotten too not long ago that Jesus fed five thousand with a little boy's lunch which consisted of two fish and five loaves of bread.

They told Jesus that they had seven loaves. Jesus commanded the people to sit down. He took the seven loaves, and He thankfully worships God the Father for the loaves. Jesus broke the bread and gave them to the disciples to distribute to them. They had a few small fish, and He worships God again by blessing the fish. The fish and the loaves began to multiply until everyone was fed and there was some leftover, Mark 8: 1 - 9.

In the Old Testament, we had seen similar miracles when the meal and the oil were multiplying because the widow of Zarephath worshipped God through obedience by obeying Elijah, the prophet of God. She did what he asked her to do, and God blessed her greatly 1 King 17: 12-15.

The 18th Miracle supports my idea that there is an excellent correlation between worship and miracles. To beg God in all sincerity is to worship Him in the Spirit of the truth. In this miracle, we find a man who was searching for Jesus. When he saw Him, he begged on behalf of his only child for healing. According to the Bible, his son was in lousy shape caused by an evil Spirit, which happened to be a devil. The man was as honest as he could be and confessed to Jesus how he went to the disciples to cast out the Spirit, but they could not do it. Jesus was disappointed that they were not able to drive the Spirit away from the boy. Jesus referred to them as a faithless and perverse generation, and He asked them to bring the boy to Him. His father did just that, and Jesus rebuked that unclean Spirit, healed the boy, and gave him back to his father. Almost everyone was amazed by the mighty power of God, Luke 9: 37 - 43.

The disciples, did they have the capabilities to cast out devils? The answer is yes, but the condition of their hearts would not allow them to operate in this gift. Their unbelieving hearts, their judgmental minds, and their criticisms of others had quenched the gift. I firmly believe that wherever and by whomever God miracles have performs, the presence of doubt will always be at the scene. Be sure that you are not the one who doubts the Holy Ghost or the Holy Spirit through vain jealousy while He is working through someone else in a way that is unfamiliar to you. The universality of these issues has become scary and confusing because it is difficult to tell who is on God's side. The way we fight against each other over power to impress man religiously. These behaviors are taking a toll on sincere believers of God. What is so hard about this formula? If I am operating in the name of Jesus or Holy Trinity, that means we are not against each other. We are on the same team but with different skills, with common goals to lodge with God eternally in heaven.

The 19th Miracle was about two blind men who had their minds made up to receive healing by the side of the road from the Healer Himself. When they heard Jesus, they were worshipping Him by praying to Him to "have mercy on them." Matthew 20: 30

This was not the first time we heard this prayer pray, but the needy received their healing from Jesus on every occasion. There is always a multitude present attempting to interfere with their healing business between them and God. These experiences should bring to mind the operation of today's Christian Church's denomination.

The multitude wanted them to shut up, but they kept on going, crying after their healing. The two blind men must have learned something that we should know, and that is the perseverance of worship often brings satisfactory results of hearts desires. Jesus called and asked them what they wanted Him to do for them. They asked Him to open their eyes, and He did full of compassion. Again, where worship is sincere and truthful, there abide miracles, signs, and wonders. The difference between worship and praise is that not anyone can worship God, but anyone can praise God if the worship is proper, so the praise. Because the sincerity of the praise depends on the true nature of worship.

The 20th Miracle dealt with a man that was deaf and had a speech impediment. They brought him to Jesus to lay hands on him. Jesus took him away from the multitude because He was about to do something many would not understand, and many would think it was nasty. Jesus put His fingers into his ears, and He spat and touched the man's tongue. Then Jesus looked up toward heaven, toward His Father, which was a worship moment, and He commanded the ears and the mouth to open, and they did, Mark 7: 31-35.

Here comes the word of faith. Whenever we beseech God, we will never go wrong, and this is what worship is all about.

The 21ˢᵗ Miracle was concerning a blind man whom they led to Jesus for a special touch to receive his eyes sights. Jesus was in town when they brought him. Jesus took him by his hand and led him out of town from the midst of the unbelievers. Then, Jesus's spat in his eyes and touched it. When did Jesus ask him did, he see anything? The blind man looked up and saw men as trees walking. Here comes the power of worship again, Jesus a second time touched his eyes, made him look up, and he was recovered from his blindness, Mark 8: 22-25.

As worshippers, we should never ignore the power of looking up.

The 22ⁿᵈ Miracle was about a blind man again, but he was a beggar. He heard the people passing by, he inquired as to what was happening, and they told him it was Jesus passing by. The blind man did not waste any time to go after his healing by praying to Jesus for mercy. The people rebuked him, but the more he cried to the Lord until his supplication to receive his sight reached the ears of Jesus. Then Jesus healed him according to his faith, Luke 18: 35-42.

As worshippers of God, we should not allow anyone to dictate to us when to address God and go after our blessing. Remember again, worship is a personal affair, and one may never understand why we worship God the way we do, especially when one is not walking in our shoes. In worship, perseverance is the key to success.

The 23rd Miracle was concerning Simon Peter, who toiled all night and had not caught any fish. Jesus, in the meantime, was teaching the people. When the class was over, He told Simon Peter to launch his nets to the deep for a draught. Simon Peter explained to Jesus his failure to catch anything that day but cast the nets to please Him. He did, and the launch was successful. His net could not hold all the fish that he enclosed, and the net broke. Simon Peter called on his partners to come to help bring the fish to the shore. When Simon Peter saw all the fish, he took conscience of his unbelief. He fell at Jesus's feet and worshiped Him with a sorrowful heart, Luke 5: 1-9.

What we need to know on this Christian journey is to doubt God is a crime against worship.

The 24th Miracle was concerning the widow's son who died, and she was left alone. Near the gate of the city, Jesus met a man carrying away her dead son, and many people were with her. Jesus had compassion for her and asked her not to weep. Then Jesus commanded the young man to arise, and he emerged from the dead and started to talk. As a result, there was an invasion of fear on all, and they began to worship and praise God, Luke 7:11 - 16.

We must glorify God for others' deliverance and our own because redemption through worship comes from God's compassion.

The 25th Miracle was about a woman who had a Spirit of infirmity for eighteen years. According to the Bible, Jesus was teaching in the synagogue on the Sabbath when He saw the woman. She was bowed together and was unable to lift herself. When Jesus called her and laid hands on her immediately, she became straight glorifying God. The ruler of the synagogue got angry instead of helping her worshiping God for her deliverance. He was furious with Jesus for healing her on the Sabbath day. He called himself using his power to warn the people about Jesus' misconduct in the synagogue. Jesus showed them how hypocritical they could be in the affairs of God. Jesus shamed them all, and the people rejoiced for all the glorious things done by Jesus, Luke 13:10 - 17.

Why is it so hard for worshippers of God and the unbelievers to understand every day is a day that sanctifies for miracles, signs, and wonders? We better not let anyone distract us enough to cause us to miss out on our miracles, signs, and wonders through authentic worship.

In the 26th Miracle, we found Jesus in the house of one of the chief Pharisees to eat bread on a Sabbath, quite a blessing that should have been for the chief and his crew if they were not so busy watching Jesus for the wrong reason. There was man who had dropsy, came to Jesus on on the Sabbath Day and He healed him regardless of what they thought of Him, Luke 14:1 - 6.

This miracle rings the bell on the fact about the Sabbath day. Whatever day that is, it set aside to fellowshipping with God but for those who are also bound to make free by God.

The 27th miracle was about ten lepers who stood far away and worshiped Jesus with these words, "Jesus, Master, have mercy on us," Luke 11:13. As the story continued, Jesus saw them and said to the ten lepers, "Go show yourselves unto the priests." The minute the lepers departed to see the priest, and they were healed, Luke 17:14.

Why did Jesus send them to show themselves unto the priest? Keep in mind, Jesus sent them to the priest to show respect for the Mosaic Law, which I elaborated on earlier in a previous chapter because whoever healed from leprosy must show themselves to the priests.

One of the lepers came back glorifying God after realizing that he was healed. Loud and fell at Jesus's feet and worshipped Him through thanksgiving, and he was a Samaritan. He was the only one who came back. The other nine were not anywhere to be found. The least among them was the one who went back to glorified God for his healing.

Worshippers of God, here's a little advice, always be the one to come back to worship and praise God with thanksgiving and gladness for whatever he does for us. "Lord have mercy upon me" This prayer healed many people throughout the Bible, and it is still an effective prayer today. I remembered finding myself in a challenging situation, a situation that had the potential to steal, kill, and destroy both my character and my integrity. My horrible ordeals ushered me into a state of depression. My dilemma was so profound that affecting my prayer life to express it better my worship life. By the way, both are the same. It was appearing to me that the whole wide world chose to believe falsehoods against me. Some of my Christian friends and colleagues were teamed up against me in the midst of my trouble without considering my character and my integrity. They started to celebrate my predicament. Little did they know, even though my prayers appetite had left me, I was able to regain what was stolen from me with these golden words of worship, "Lord have mercy on me." He heard me, and He granted my request just like He has done for those in The Old and The New Testament. Since that day, He made a covenant with me to make anew His mercies for me daily.

Worshippers of God, I can't stress enough how important it is to store up as many prayers as we can while we are strong because it is those prayers that will sustain us in our time of weakness.

The 28th Miracle deals with the High priest's servant's right ear smote by one of the disciples, and Jesus touched his ear and healed him, Luke 22:50, 51.

To protect the purity of your worship, worshippers of God, never hold grudges against anyone and turn everything in God's hands, including malicious Spiritual criticism.

The 29th Miracle was about the nobleman's son who was sick to the point of death. When the nobleman came to Jesus on behalf of his son for healing, instead of Jesus went to his house, He sent the nobleman back home with the guarantee he would find his son well. He believed Jesus instantly, John 4: 46-54.

The boy's father was a nobleman in his society, but spiritually speaking, we as worshippers and believers of God are noble, virtuous, and particular people.

The nobleman had faith in Jesus, and he was not the only one among those who received the healing from our Savior through worship who demonstrated great faith. They all did in a way. How do I know that? Without some confidence in God, there is rarely a Godly breakthrough. To have faith in God requires obedience because obedience is what brings faith to its maturity. Let me push the issue a little further to obey God's word is to love and have faith in Him. Most of the recipients of the miracles demonstrate their faith through their actions and words, depicting their love for Jesus the compassionate Healer. Through their sincere worship and praise, they got the victory in Christ our Lord. I said, "Most Miracles" because I was not sure about the nine leprous who did not come back to worship

Jesus with thanksgiving for their healing as the tenth one did. Please, worshippers of God, never forget to worship God with "Thanks," Saying thank you to God who has the power to keep the windows of heaven wide open so blessings can continually pour out on the thankful.

CHAPTER TEN

NO WORSHIP, NO MIRACLES

By now, I believe the point is well taken; there are no miracles without some form of worshipping God. Worship is what determines our relationships with God and how much we love Him. Worship is what engages us in frank conversation with God. To pray, beg, fear, love, seek, believe, and praise God cover most of the territories of worship.

Again, worship activates all miracles, including personal ones, and personal unbelief is what deactivates personal miracles. As worshippers of God, to allow anyone to make you believe in the existence of today's miracles is a crime against the anointing of God upon His believers. Let me push the above statement a little further, it is a form of blasphemy against the Holy Ghost, or the Holy Spirit take your pick to avoid the vain argument, which is the trick of the distracter to keeping us from concentrating on more serious matters such as walking in our anointing. Exercising of our authority against the devil through the working of miracles, signs, and wonders is to beware of worship and miracles killers who at times consider themselves to be worshippers of God as well, but they deny His miracle working power religiously. I wish they could have learned of the danger of spreading their ideologies around because for a seasoned believer to demonstrate unbelief in the existence of today's miracle is a crime against a baby believer.

Let us glance at the 30th Miracle to see if we can detect the activation of worship. This miracle involves a cripple man by the pool of Bethesda. He had been sick for thirty-eight years. He desired to get in the pool for healing, but he had too many obstacles in his way to make it happen. First of all, he would need someone to usher him in the water whenever the angel troubled the water, and he must be the first one to jump in because the healing always went to the first jumper. It appeared there was no hope for him because all the others that were waiting for the angel to stir up the water were better fit and most likely to be first to jump in the water. He knew all of this, but still, he kept on coming to the pool expecting. His patience and his determination had paid off when he met Jesus. Our Savior asked him a question, he answered by sharing his plaint with Jesus. He could not have chosen a better Person to pour out his heart to besides our Savior. Jesus moved by compassion and commanded him to rise and pick up his bed and walk. Immediately the impotent man was healed indeed, John 5:1- 8.

This impotent man had defeated all discouragements that could create a negative impact on his healing. Amid the obstacles, he chose to embrace patience, one of the most impressive attributes of worship a child of God could ever possess. I often say the worshippers who wait patiently to hear from the Lord have no other choice but to have a prosperous life and soul. I am about to point out an observation that should not be taken lightly, most of Jesus' miracles took place on a particular day, "The Sabbath Day." Today we are still observing the Sabbath regardless of the confusion and the distraction arising around it as far as which day of the week is supposed to be the Sabbath Day. In my opinion, this too is absurd for worshippers to engage in such argument Monday through Sunday; take your pick. However, whatever day or days one chooses for the Sabbath Day, keep it holy that is what impresses God. It is a day of thanksgiving, a day to work miracles, signs, and wonders, a day for deliverance, a day to be blessed, a day to listen and to obey God's voice, a day to do good, a day to come closer and closer to God.

In summary, it is a day sanctify to worship. Sorry, am I talking about every day of the week? Yes, I'm, and I will not apologize for it, but let us say your Church or Assembly choose Friday, Saturday, or Sunday as their Sabbath Day; this is their prerogative. It is also a Covenant between you, the organization, and God that everyone agrees to set this particular day aside as their seventh day of the week as it was commanded by God to keep it Holy. Let us go back to my observation; most of Jesus's miracles that we read in the Bible took place on the Sabbath Day. I know, and I believe that Jesus is still working miracles today, but how many of us miss our miracles for playing hooky from Church on our Sabbath Day frequently? One time could be too many if the reason for our "M I A" (Missing in Action) is not validated by God. Worshippers of God must be there at your post of worship on your Sabbath Day in your synagogue because God expects you to be there. Let me end this miracle with this advice. God does not like to be stood up by His main worshippers, who is you and me. Can God count on us to be in worship service if everybody else decides to stay away from Church on the Sabbath Day? In worship, we can't depend on or expect everyone to fill in our gap. When I was coming up, my brother and I decided to raise a goat back in my country. Believe it or not, the goat was starving to death. How could that happen? We both thought that we loved the goat, but our actions proved different. It was simple, I depended on my brother to feed the goat, and he counted on me to do the same. I thought he was feeding our poor goat, and he thought I was too, and at the end of the day, no one provided for the goat, and it died. We became angry at each other, and neither of us was willing to take the blame for the death of our goat. The argument between us was so heated until he and I agreed to take the matter to our mother to be the judge. That was the greatest mistake we ever made because after she listened to both of us, she rendered her verdict with a whip and whipped both of us, and I have the scar to prove it. We did not have a DSS (Department Social Service) to report child abuse cases, but if we had a DSS, my mother was equipped enough to whip that idea of calling DSS out of us. I thanked God for the beating. It brought my brother and me to our senses. We realized we were both guilty as charged. Since then, I grew up believing I instead overdo it rather than not doing it and never depend on anyone else to fulfill my obligation while I can do it.

The 31st Miracle was about a man who was blind from birth. The disciples wanted to know who sinned to cause this blindness on the man, him, or his parents. Jesus told them neither one had sinned. It happened for the works, plural, of God should be manifested on him. With spit and dirt, made clay, anointed the blind man's eyes, and sent him to wash his face. He went and did what was commanded of him to do. The blind man received his sight through obedience. Jesus also did this miracle on Sabbath Day, John 9: 1- 18.

No worship, no miracles because worship and miracles are in love with obedience, obedience to follow God's direction and teaching.

Worshippers of God, in other to receive and offer miracles, we must learn how to be submissive unto God's voice and His instructions.

The 32nd Miracle depicted the raising of Lazarus from the dead. When Jesus knew that Lazarus was dead, He was on his way to Lazarus and his sisters' house. One of the sisters, Martha was her name saw Jesus, and she ran, fell at His feet, and worshipped Him. Martha told Him that if He were there, her brother would not have died. She added that even now, whatever Jesus would ask God, God would grant it to Him. Jesus promised her that her brother would rise again, but Martha thought He was speaking on the resurrection on the last day. As the conversation went on Jesus gave her a faith test, and she passed it. Then Jesus went where they laid Lazarus, and there, He worshiped His Father, and His father permitted Him the permission to raise Lazarus from the dead, and He did it. According to Jesus's prayer, Martha did know what she was talking about concerning Jesus and His Father, quite an inseparable relationship.

I must stop right here discussing the miracles. However, it was not my intention to quit right here, but please understand that I am a salesclerk, and God is my CEO, and He told me to go to the conclusion of this worship and praise.

No worship, no miracles, and this idea might as well welcome all the attractions of controversies and criticisms based on the right to agree and disagree. The meaning of worship for a true believer should be praying and talking to God all earnestly and sincerity of heart. I am forced to play with words here to bring more light to this meaning of worship, but the absolute fact of the matter is to pray to God is to talk to God vice versa. In doing so, worship comes in effect, and praise becomes indispensable.

Average believers are worshipping God at least three times or more daily. If the question was asked of them how many times they worship in a week, do not be surprised if the answer would be once a week. Referring to Friday, Saturday, or Sunday worship gatherings depends on your organization. I will take full responsibility for the statement I am about to make, and there is no other way to address or communicate with God other than worship because of His holiness. Keep in mind, when having an excellent and satisfactory prayer life based on God's establishment of miracles, signs, and wonders would become elements of your worship moments. I often hear believers saying they are expecting a blessing from God. To expect something from God is the feeling coming from a request previously made to God through worship. When the expectation through faith becomes a reality giving praises to God is inevitable, but it all starts with prayer.

The conclusion of this matter is never let anyone shy away from the kind of worship that God expects from you. Remember again, and it is a personal affair. No two worshippers worship alike. One may introduce the other to worship still. At the end of the day, there will be a difference in their worship. Life for true believers is all about worship. I often hear in my religious circles that everything is in the praise; I am in total disagreement with this belief because I believe that everything is in worship. Worship is what ushers us out of our situations and dilemmas, making our soul free to give praise to God Almighty. We cannot let anyone modify our giving ways of worship to satisfy their ego. Remember, the anointing of God in a worship place does not come upon anyone just to come. He always has a mission. Could the task be carried out the way that the commission received without interference?

Remember, the Bible, regardless of The Old and The New Testaments, is One God's book. We can't let anyone stop us from going after our miracles. Man's wisdom teaches or attempts to teach us there is no such thing as faith healings, and some gifts disappeared forever. "The devil is a liar," God is the same yesterday, today, and tomorrow which report are we going to believe man or God's. I, I prefer to follow God's report blindfolded. Whatever we must go on with us and in us, let us introduce them to worship because worship is the solution for everything in humankind's life.

Let us spend more time reading and studying those instructions found in our survival kit, the Bible. Many believers and unbelievers have misunderstood this book. With believers, we want to add to it, and with unbelievers, they refute knowledge.

As believers of God, we need to be more compassionate to those entrapped by Satan's various tricks. We need to understand our position in this matter. We, as the church, need to display our Christianity daily. It seems that today's church is geared more toward exposing other's infirmities than embracing the One who does and continues doing amazing things in our lives, our Lord and Savior Jesus Christ. We need to adopt a Spirit of humility to restore and help those who departed from the faith and those who think they are unfit to be among us. Listen, we are all sinful men and women, and the difference between the saved and unsaved is Jesus, and with Jesus, no one needs to die unsaved, but it will take you and me to make this secret known to them who do not accept Him. The difference between heaven and hell is an exception. If one accepts Jesus for who He is as a Son of God, heaven belongs to him; if one does not believe in Jesus, hell belongs to him. This is the most straightforward formula I can develop, and I pray it will find root in the heart.

I am leaving these two quotations with you. "For all have sinned, and come short of the Glory of God;" Romans 3:23

"For the wages of sin is death; but the gift of God is eternal life through Jesus Christ our Lord." Romans 6:23.

Saints of God, let us examine ourselves or let us reason together. Are we making disciple our business win souls through strife, negative criticism, and vain competition among us created by diverse religious belief on the idea "MINE IS BETTER THAN YOURS?" Let us be patient in the meantime, let the wheat and the tares grow together, and at the end of the season, God Himself will separate them. Let us evangelize and make disciples for our Lord, and at the end, we will be the sheep, not the goat and the vines that bear good fruits. Do not get me wrong; I understand the hardship of not being able to criticize each other's belief in the word of God. Criticism could be either constructive or negative, and both tend to make or tear up potentially serious believers. Therefore, we do need to approach our criticism toward others with caution, especially when it comes to the affairs of God, before ending up criticizing the manifestation of the Holy Ghost or the Holy Spirit in believers, which is a form of blasphemy. Look what happened in the Gospel of John Chapter 10:19 – 21. There was a division among the Jews for these sayings, and many of them said, He hath a devil, and is mad; why hear ye him? Others said these are not the words of him that hath a devil. Can a devil open the eyes of the blind?

In this scripture, the Jews did not use any caution, but others did and thanked God. Let me start paraphrasing some of the statements made By Jesus in Chapter 10 of the same Gospel of John to conclude, "Worship is not an option, but a requirement." We see the Jews after they saw all the things that our Savior did. They still wanted to know if he was, He the Christ, and Jesus answered them by pointing out their problems, which reminds me of our difficulties today regarding each other. Jesus told them, but they believed not the works that Jesus did in His Father's name; they bear witness of Him. He said the reason for their unbelief was since they were not a part of Him. They did not know Him. (John 10: 25, 26) I am doing injustice to this chapter by quoting or paraphrasing a few verses from it; please, worshippers of God, read this Chapter 10 of the Gospel of John. It will enhance your faith through worship and praise. However, we must learn to understand and respect other's religious beliefs through Christ our

Lord. Remember this: "And other sheep I have, which are not of this fold: then also I must bring, and they shall hear my voice; and there shall be one fold, and one shepherd." John 10:16

In the meantime, let us worship God in the Spirit, and truth, this is our duty. Worship and praise God with all our being.

THANK GOD FOR OBEDIENCE.